LIVE IN THE Q

The Axiom for Work and Life

How to Be
"The Most Perfect Embodiment
of [You] in [Your] Purest Form"
Before Lunch!

By Mike Forsyth, Ph.Q.

Includes:
11 workplace challenges
addressed by Q-ism

Live in the Q^{TM}, Quintessentialism^{TM}, Quintessentialism Cycle^{TM}, Quintessentialism Process^{TM}, Q-ism^{TM}, Q-Zone^{TM}, Count the Qs^{TM}, See to Be^{TM}, Me-Zone^{TM}, We-Zone^{TM} are trademarks of Mike Forsyth and www.mikeforsyth.com

eBook ISBN: 978-1-7329179-1-0
Paperback ISBN: 978-1-7329179-0-3

Cover design: Sophia Scott
www.Fiverr.com

Website developer: Alex Agherbi
alex.agherbi@gmail.com

Author photo: Jennifer Barnes
jenniferbarnesphotography.com

DEDICATION

To Uncle Dave and Aunt Kathleen--
For the invitation you extended to me over 30 years ago.

And to Coles and Rieske -
For being the quintessence of living in the Q that weekend.
Here's another thank-you to add to the pile.

ACKNOWLEDGEMENTS

To my wife, Lisa—
who's never liked the smooth and sappy movie lines.
Let's try this instead:
"Of all the blessings that can be held and stuff,
you are my greatest holdable one."
I love you! Thank you!

To my family—
when one succeeds, we ALL succeed. Because it took us all to make
this happen! You've sacrificed a lot.
I love you. Thank you!

To Mom and Dad—
"Look at the book I wrote!" I shout
while hopping off the school bus, running inside to throw it on the
kitchen table, and then running back out to play.
(Your happy boy stands forever on the shoulders of your love and
sacrifice.) Thank you!

To my editor, K. Cottrell—
How fun was this, huh? Fate brought us together! I had no idea how
much I needed an editor. I could not have done this without you!
Thank you!

FORWARD

Wahoo! It's my very first forward! Oh, yeah.
It's my first book too.
This thing started writing itself. I guess it was time.

Five weeks later, here it is.
Not perfect, not complete, not the final.
But finished!

Now, onto the next challenge that lies beyond
my comfort zone.

I'm getting used to this!

GLOSSARY

ax·i·om \ ˈaksēəm \ *noun*
1. "A statement or proposition which is regarded as being established, or self-evidently true."
2. "A statement that is taken to be true, to serve as a premise or starting point for further reasoning and arguments."
3. "A self-evident or universally recognized truth; a maxim"

quin·tes·sen·tial \ kwin-tə-ˈsen(t)-shəl \ *noun*
1. "The essence of a thing in its purest and most concentrated form"
2. Of or relating to "the most perfect embodiment of something"
3. "The most nearly perfect manifestation of a quality or thing"

quin·tes·sen·tial·*ism* \ kwin-tə-ˈsen(t)-shəl-izəm \ *noun*
1. A breakthrough explanation for how one is "the essence of [oneself] in [one's] purest...form".
2. Discovering and being "the most perfect embodiment of [oneself]"
3. Celebrating "the most nearly perfect manifestation of [you]" achieved (today--before lunch!) when living quintessentially; also referred to as "*living in the Q*"

quin·tes·sen·tial·*ist* \ kwin-tə-ˈsen(t)-shəl-əst \ *noun*
1. One who strives to be "the essence of [oneself] in [one's] purest... form"
2. An individual discovering and being "the most perfect embodiment of [themselves]"
3. Any person who celebrates "the most nearly perfect manifestation of [themselves]"; achieved (today--before lunch!) when living quintessentially; also referred to as "*living in the Q*"

TABLE OF CONTENTS

Section Two: The Addendum for Work and Life

Section One:

THE AXIOM FOR WORK AND LIFE

CHAPTER 1
The Quintessential Tease – Setting the Stage for Q-ism

Isms are Incomplete

Hello there, reader! Glad you've joined me! Like Movies? Grab the popcorn because here we GO!

A Beautiful Mind, 2002's Academy Award-winning Best Picture of the Year (seen it?) is a favorite flick of mine, with insights and connections from which I've continued to draw for years. Wouldn't have guessed though, that I'd be using it to start my first book! (Lucky for you--it was almost *Napoleon Dynamite*, until a few minutes ago.)

Played by Russell Crowe and inspired by the esteemed life of John Nash, this gifted Nobel Laureate in Economics began his university pursuits at Princeton. While there, he struggled to find a breakthrough of scholastic merit worth publication. UNTIL HE DID! And did so in a moment of pure epiphany to boot! During the scene when a light bulb turned on in his mind, he says to his classmates around him, "Adam Smith (known worldwide as the father of modern economics) needs revision!" He states further that one of Smith's foundational premises was "incomplete"!

Kinda like minimalism. (And every other ISM!)

I am a self-proclaimed minimalist. I don't know if anyone loves throwing things out or giving things away more than me. Cleaning out the garage is nourishment to my soul. A perfect day might well include going through the game closet! (True story: my family and I once did just that as part of my birthday celebration.) I daydream of living out of a suitcase. I have checked prices on prefabricated homes (please don't tell my wife and kids) and I think it would be so darn cool if every document, picture or historical artifact of mine was living in the cloud, and digitized on a thumb drive hanging from a thin rope around my neck.

Yes, I love the idea of minimizing. But regarding the underlying purpose to our living every day, minimalism – is incomplete. It doesn't get us to the *ultimate why*. It can only be a means to something more. And like realism, activism, conservationism, botulism--minimalism is not the *end*. (Okay, maybe botulism.)

We minimalists seek to minimize our lives for many reasons, some of which are merely to cope with the stresses and demands of a hectic life: to slow down, to feel more present, less distracted, free from the demands that all this stuff we collect can have upon us. Indeed, these reasons do have merit and benefit. Noble pursuits to be sure. But WHY be less busy, less in a hurry? WHY slow it down at all? At the conclusion of a good, long wardrobe wrestle that ends with stuffed bags for charity, we should have a *final* WHY and be able to articulate it.

We should also know our ultimate END and understand it. We should know how throwing shirts away got us closer to that end, if at all. Otherwise, we're eventually sitting in our new tiny house, with only the clothes we have on, looking around proudly, twiddling our thumbs, and are no more clear on the answer to, "I did all this becauuuse…?"
"To simplify!"
"Excellent! I love to simplify. Becauuuse?"
"It helps me relax!"
"Great! Relaxing is wonderful! So, you can?
"Better enjoy each day!"

"Awesome answer! And enjoying each day helps you to?"
"...uh... live?"
"Yes! To live! And you're living life because...?"

. . . .

And as if this deeper, ultimate WHY and END for our lives weren't hard enough to grasp and articulate, here's another question that has some 'splaining' to do!

What exactly, does it look like to BE our BEST SELF? (Ever asked yourself that question?) When are you your *very* best? To many—uh, to MOST?—this is as unfathomably ambiguous, remarkably relative, and 'quite possibly too impossible' a question to answer.
. . . .

No more! Days wondering about what constitutes our ultimate *why* and *end* will soon be behind us! **There IS an ultimate end and a why to describe!** And feeling stumped on the question of when you are unequivocally your *very best you*? **The answer is only a few pages away!**

Yes! There is an end and a why to *every* ISM! *This* ISM! **Q-ism!**

And there is a way to articulate when you're living at your very best! It's *this* living – **Q living!**

And the beauty of all of this – is that it's simple, doable and possible – *before lunch!*

. . . .

Later on, in *A Beautiful Mind*, Russell Crowe's character, John Nash, confidently hands his finished thesis to his professor for review. After glancing carefully at the pages, the professor looks up and says to John, "You do realize this flies in the face of 150 years of economic theory? That's rather presumptuous, don't you think?"

"It is sir," John replies.

Whether this little book even makes the smallest ripple in conventional thought, let alone flies in the face of years of metaphysics and ontology, we'll let you and history decide. I won't hold my breath. But... I am very excited about, and indeed do believe that what I'm writing about needs a voice!

The ultimate *why* and the *end* to all our means needs clarification and definition. It needs simplification and articulation. Like John Nash to Adam Smith, "it's incomplete."
And describing what it truly means to *be our best selves*, to ourselves — needs revision!

A Billion Things Just Disappeared!

Who doesn't love an incredible magic trick? No one looks away when our reality and our senses are being defied before our very eyes! We are forced to question *everything!*

And the best magicians do it oh so well! Imagine for a moment the mysteriously captivating illusionist waving hands and snapping fingers over a hidden object resting very still underneath a red box on a small table. All eyes are fixed. All breathing has stopped. The audience is silent when the box is lifted and gasps become hoorays when instantly the bread once visible from the top of the toaster, has now completely disappeared!

Even more gasps from the dismayed crowed when the illusionist holds up the power cord to reveal that the toaster... wasn't even PLUGGED IN!

As hard as it is to say, I think I've got a better one! Believe it or not, I can make a *billion* EXTERNAL VARIABLES completely *disappear!* Check this out:

<u>IF</u> being our *best selves*, (an idea I'm on a quest to redefine) is possible for every one of us, (and not just *likely*, but genuinely possible *today*, as I believe to be the case) <u>THEN</u> extraordinarily, the billions of things that are different between every single person on Earth, must by necessity be mostly irrelevant.

And <u>IF</u> the ultimate *end* and *why* can be found within our schedules for *today*, <u>THEN</u> the billions of differences between your calendar or agenda and mine, and everyone's, must wistfully vanish away... into the shiny silver toaster of life.

If the final end and why to living can happen *now*, then fulfilling our purpose must *not* be conditioned upon where we are at this moment. If each of us *can* be our very best today, then it *mustn't* be dependent upon the place we call home, the transportation we use, the food we eat, the language we speak, the clothes we wear, the things we buy, the places we go and the books we read. It can't be contingent upon the medals we've earned, the money we've saved, the accomplishments we've made, the Twitter followers we have, the tasks we've completed and the years we've lived. (And. a billion. other. things.)

But it does...
Have something to do...
With those...
We...

Are…
With.

Keep reading! This magic show has only just BEGUN!

What We DO vs. Who We ARE

NFL coaches are smart! There's only 32 in the world. When one agrees with you – take note!

Earlier this year, I caught a few minutes of sports radio host Colin Cowherd as he interviewed former Arizona Cardinals Head Coach Bruce Arians. Bruce had just retired and seemed well relaxed; pleased to be visiting about the world of the National Football League and his experience as one of its coaches for many years. What comes next is a distinction made by Bruce, between two individuals. Place your focus here, and watch what unfolds.

Paraphrasing all of this to the best of my memory, Colin asked Coach Arians, "In your opinion, having worked so closely with so many, who of all the *players* that you have ever coached, was the *best?*" Colin tried helping him out by listing a couple names of well-known stars that he assumed would be candidates for his answer. Bruce responded with a name that I'm sure NO ONE would have guessed. It certainly wasn't one I recognized, and Colin seemed surprised as well. The last name was Palmer. Bruce said he'd coached him years ago, and that he played two years in the league and said something to the effect of, 'Regarding pure *athleticism*, pound for pound, he was the best *player* I've ever coached.'

Colin responded with, "Interesting; I thought you were going to name Larry Fitzgerald." (Larry is currently a well-known 11-time Pro Bowler and wide receiver for the Arizona Cardinals.)

It was then that Mr. Arians said something that needs repeating. And considering how it struck me, I think I'm pretty close to word for word when he said, "Now, best *player*—that would be Palmer. Best *person*? Larry Fitzgerald **is the best *person* I've ever known**." He further stated, "There's a distinction there. Being a great football *player* (Palmer) and being a great *person* (Larry Fitzgerald) are two different things."

(Long pause for emphasis here.)

What is it then, that makes a great football *player* also a great *person*?

What is it that makes a great zookeeper, coach, clerk, plumber, lawyer, doctor, singer, songwriter, sweeper, sawyer, chef, shrink, son or daughter, mother, father... a great *person*? I claim it can be defined! Simply. Understandably. Vague responses cut it no longer!

We're on a journey to understand what it MEANS to be our *best selves*; and what MAKES us our best selves. With about a gazillion different places we need to be, or vocations in the world — it's clear that what we DO, doesn't always speak for who we ARE.

These many different jobs--they're just another external variable that quietly disappears as we discuss what matters most, that of *being* our very best - in any and all circumstances. And knowing the difference between doing the "do" and being the "be," opens the door to achieving our potential - today!

Hold on! Things are getting interesting!

"Quinta – Whaaat?"
A New Word is Born
(Quintessentialism)

"What did you say? Quinta-supercalifragi--what?"

Imagine Daniel LaRusso from *The Karate Kid* asking that of Mr. Miyagi, as he runs to catch up with him. "What kind of a word is that!? It better not mean: 'paint the house!'"

"DANIEL-san!" (Now it's clear I'm no Mr. Miyagi, but stay with me! Your 'Wax On/Wax Off' will thank you.)

Yes, I know--it's a long word. But it's **Quintessentialism**. (Kwin-tuh-sen-chil-is-um!) It's a word that means something that...well,...I can't wait to define for the world!

It's only a word because I've invented it. Quintessentialism doesn't exist in any dictionary--yet! There's *quintessence*, and there's *quintessential*, but there isn't *quintessentialism*. Except here, and until now! And like I said, I can't wait to define it! It has everything to do with what we've been discussing so far.

Yes! Another ISM is about to be born! But THIS one is the ism that *surrounds* all other isms! It's what I propose to be the *biggest* ism, and the most *essential* ism... of all. It's the end and why to *every* ism. It's at the heart of what it means to be our very best!

A quick search online for the definition of 'quintessence' will pull up: "the *most perfect* or typical example of a quality or class." Here's another: "The *perfect embodiment* of some*thing*" or "The most *nearly perfect manifestation* of a quality or thing." One more, and it's my favorite: "The *essence of a thing* in its *purest* and *most concentrated* form." I grabbed a couple of uses of the word in sentences off the internet as well:

● Tanya has always been the **quintessence** of *high fashion*, so I was taken aback when I saw her wearing an old, saggy pair of jeans and a ragged T-shirt.

● These chocolate bars are the **quintessence** of delicious *treats* for the soul.

● For many children and adolescents all over the world, the name Voldemort is the **quintessence** of *evil*.

● Benjamin Franklin must have been the **quintessence** of *self-improvement* because he made a list of thirteen critical virtues and tracked his progress in abiding by the index.

To you who are reading this right now, and to the entire world as well, I have a question!

What is the "most perfect," or "most nearly perfect," "embodiment," or "manifestation" of YOU?

What is the *"essence"* of **YOU** in **YOUR** *"purest form?"*

What is... your *best self*?

What is the quintessence of (insert your name here)?

Wouldn't it do us well to pause for a MONTH on that one question alone? We absolutely could!

. . . .

Quintessential*ism* is, (*drum roll please*) discovering and being the *essence* of **oneself** in one's *purest form*.

A quintessential*ist* is one who strives to see and to be the most *perfect embodiment* of his or her self, attaining to their purpose and achieving their potential.

And the most glorious news about Quintessentialism of all?

Discovering, or *seeing* what our best self is, and then *being* our *best self...* doesn't happen at the end of a lifetime. It can happen for you and me NOW, before lunch even! No matter where you happen to be, or how old you are, or how little you may think you've done, or how far you may think you have yet to go, finding yourself in that wonderfully magical and fulfilling place--*where you truly are your very best self, answering to the biggest and brightest purposes within you* --might just happen seconds from now;

...when the next person in your life walks into your office with a question; or turns your face with their tiny, three-year-old hands; or texts you to grab some dinner on the way home.

How, do you ask?

As Mr. Miyagi said with a bow to Daniel-san in the Karate Kid; ("Always look eye!") I say it now to you, softly, slowly, lovingly, and with a smile.

"Come back tomorrow."

(Or turn the page.)

Purpose & Potential--
On Jeopardy!™

"Well, I must say Mike," announces Alex Trebek, "In my 30 plus years of hosting *Jeopardy!*™, we have never had a contestant win the theoretical maximum amount possible in the first two rounds! $283,200![1] Astonishing, to say the least!"

"I appreciate that Alex. It certainly didn't hurt to be playing against this amazingly talented and lovely mime, and of course, Mr. Goldfish over there."

"But still," responds Alex, "you had to give the correct question to *every* answer, and luckily have those Daily Doubles be the last answers remaining on the board each round!"

"You're making me blush Alex, but please remember - this is my book I'm writing this into! The very first chapter even. I'm trying to make a point right from the start. Go big, or go home, isn't that what they say?"

"I guess so," laughs Alex. "That does explain how you knew the answer '7 - 35 - 10.'"

"What was my locker combination in 9th grade?" Mike follows with a smile. The audience laughs.

"Heading into commercial break, here's the clue for *Final Jeopardy!*™ Mike, to help determine how much you want to wager: (ding goes the screen) *'The Purpose of Life.'* Think that over for a minute and we'll be back right after this."

---

[1] https://bit.ly/2yaF3KA

It wasn't long before Alex was reading the final answer to our lone contestant: "*'The world-acclaimed book,* Live in the Q, *asserts that doing THIS, is the ultimate end and why to living each day.'*"

The music starts playing, but Mike is waiting with a smile through most of it. Pen down, and fingers tapping.
"Alright," says Alex, "let's see what you have."

Reading the screen in front of Mike, Alex says, "'**What is being your VERY best self?**' That is correct! And how much did you wager? All of it, WOW! Which means a grand total for today of $566,400! Absolutely staggering!"

Mike and Alex shake hands and converse pleasantly while the audience applauses in amazement. The other two contestants excitedly join them. "So--being your VERY best self. Who knew!?" exclaims Alex.

"Well, at least it's what I propose, Mr. Trebek. I like the thought that reaching our potential, by being our best, is indeed the noblest of endeavors, and truly fulfills our grandest purposes."

"How so?" The mime interrupts, demonstratively. (And silently.)

"Great question," Mike smiles. "For a lot of reasons, which I explain in my book, but for starters: what's better than best? And secondly--and this is what I believe to be so encouraging--is that it's actually more possible to be our best selves, and reach our potential than we might typically think. It doesn't happen *after* a journey of a thousand miles. Rather, it's something we can do along the journey, *every* 'mile'."

"So, the ultimate purpose to each day, is being our very best, which IS possible... today! I love it!" exclaims Alex.

"I know, right!? And what's exciting to me," Mike continues, "is that those two ideas are the answer to each other's question - like *Jeopardy!* Look at this: (*Mike starts writing on his podium screen with his pen so all can see. Alex holds up Mr. Goldfish, so he can see too.*)

- Q: What is the ultimate WHY to each day?
  A: Being our VERY best self.
- Q: When are we our VERY best self?
  A: When we are fulfilling our PURPOSE: the ultimate end and why.

Mike explains all this to the fixated friends, and then says, "I like to think of it as two sides of the same coin. The ultimate *why* and *end* on one side, (purpose) <u>is</u> being our *best self* (achieving our potential) on the other.

SIDE ONE   SIDE TWO

"So, the question then becomes," says Alex, scratching his chin, "WHEN exactly are we our *very* best, and how can we be more of it!"

"And that's exactly what my book, *Live in the Q* is all about!" exclaims Mike. "And I think many people will be pleasantly surprised at the answer!

"Quite fascinating," nods Alex. "Can't wait to read your book!"

"Can't wait to give you a signed copy," Mike says as he magically pulls one out of thin air and hands it to Alex. "Writing a book sure has its perks!"

CHAPTER 2
A Quintessential Crash! – Two Concepts Collide

Nuclear Chocolate and Peanut Butter

[CAUTION: *By reading further, you are now agreeing to the dangers of moving up and into a new dimension of Mike Forsyth's personality. It can be a bit silly, a tad more lighthearted and certainly more imaginative than you are used to. The transition can be hard for some, especially when the crux of Mike's message is one of the utmost importance. If, for any reason, you're nervous about handling his eye-rolling outlandishness juxtaposed with such consequential Quintessentialism, Mike understands and suggests that you please stop here. (Reference Mike's children's memoirs for guidance. This collection of works is entitled* Surviving Life with my Dad: Mike Forsyth.]

What is it about chocolate and peanut butter!? Harry Reese came up with the Peanut Butter Cup in 1928, and the world has never been the same. ! can tell you firsthand that it saves my wife (and many of her friends) from motherhood/wifehood/adulthood purgatory on at LEAST a weekly basis!

Just as rain and sun make rainbows, chocolate and peanut butter make happiness. Those two items came together in some form of mouth-watering magic that only the gods understand.

And... just like that sweet nectar of chocolate and peanut butter that we eat smiling (and have secretly imagined making mud pies with and then licking off our hands and fingers), the quintessence of you – or the "most perfect embodiment of you" – happens when two timeless *concepts* come together!

In fact, these two tectonic ideas, seen as separate from one another for eons--each with colossal lives of their own--come crashing together for the first time IN THIS BOOK! I know. I didn't choose Quintessentialism. Quintessentialism chose me.

And just as the marriage of peanut butter and chocolate creates happiness, these two colliding concepts create something even *better!* WAY MORE BETTER! (It's my book--I can say it how I want! After I tip my editor.)

In a way that's practically impossible to explain, the coming together of these two ideologies to form Quintessentialism is more accurately comparable to what would happen if we did more than just *mixed* chocolate and peanut butter together, say, with a spatula, **but we actually *fused* them together at the molecular level!**

You know--like scientifically! And at the famous CERN Hadron Collider on the French/Swiss border. This behemoth of a circular tunnel--six hundred feet underground, sixteen miles long and big enough for semi-trucks to drive through--is where you accelerate atomic particles to pretty much light speed and then smash them together, in order to *fuse* them together. So, imagine our particle of peanut butter and our particle of chocolate accelerated to the speed of light and then... uh yeah. You know where I'm going with this -

Quintessentialism is the joy of chocolate and peanut butter **fused into one** *at the atomic level! Nuclear* peanut butter and chocolate! $a = pc^2$ (if a is awesomeness and p is peanut butter multiplied by chocolate at the speed of light... SQUARED!!)

BIG! Awesomeness pretty much coming out of every light socket and outlet in the world!

So, what are these two tectonic concepts you ask? Keep reading!

"Live in the Now!"

When was the first time you ever encountered the phrase, "Live in the now"? The first time I heard it was while watching a movie with my high school friend one weekend our senior year. I thought it was hilarious. It turned out to be one of the most memorable moments of the entire show. We'd quote it in the cafeteria and laugh about it with our friends. Yes, it was pretty much the go-to movie for our comedic moments that year.

Do you know of which I speak? One silly rocker dude with a trucker hat and a black mullet is staring at his dream guitar through the shop window at the corner store. His friend with long blonde hair rolls up beside him with his buddies, the window of the car is down, and he says with his goofy accent and glasses, "Stop torturing yourself, man. You'll never afford it! Live in the NOW!"

Got the movie? High five! Still, don't know? Sigh. Ask your parents, kid.[2]

As a young high school student, I thought the phrase was hilarious. I thought these two comedic writers had made it up, that it was trending popular vernacular of the day. I had NO IDEA there was something more to it! And not just something more, but ancient history more!

It turns out that living in the now--this idea of being present in the today or moment of your life--is ancient Eastern philosophy to the max (originating in Asia or east of Europe). It's also dominant

---

[2] Wayne's World. (1992)

Western philosophy too--originating in ancient Greece, Europe or west of Asia).

And those two philosophical schools are pillars of thought in our universe! Age after age of world civilizations have leaned on this thinking to anchor their decision-making.

Absolutely add our day and age, and our civilization to the list! In fact, the philosophy of 'living in the now' is quickly found and recognizable within the context of today's school of thought called *mindfulness*. To illustrate this point, enjoy these quotes from a mindfulness coloring book I bought a few years back. (I'm a good colorer.)

"Most of us take for granted that time flies, meaning that it passes too quickly. But in the mindful state, time doesn't pass at all. There is only a single instant of time that keeps renewing itself over and over with infinite variety." -Deepak Chopra

"Be happy at the moment, that's enough. Each moment is all we need, not more." -Mother Teresa

"The present moment is filled with joy and happiness. If you are attentive, you will see it." -Thich Nhat Hanh

"Few of us ever live in the present. We are forever anticipating what is to come or remembering what has gone." -Louis L'Amour

"Stay present for the 'now' of your life. It is your 'point of power.'"
-Doug Dillon

Someone once said, "We should be where our feet are." Another individual said it this way, "All we have is *now*. The only place we'll ever be is *now*. Just one eternal, never-ending *now*." Summarizing mindfulness, based on the most common definitions of today, help us to see the generally accepted benefits to being solidly planted in our slippers, and noticing the eternal 'nowness around us.' Check out these timeless beauties:

First: It is best to worry less – or entirely not at all – about those things we can't control, but **focus more or even solely on the things we *can* control**. For example, worrying about the past is wasteful energy and fretting about the future isn't doing much good either, especially if that fretting stops us from taking action. Focusing on what our lives have for us today--in the present moment--is vital, and in many respects, the most reasonable way to cope and deal with the challenges of our lives.

Second: **We're always more effective when focusing on those things in front of us.** Thinking about work, when you're on vacation *from* work doesn't make any sense. Thinking about vacation, when you should be working isn't too productive either (says your manager – *for the tenth time, already*)! When we're home, our minds wander back to problems at the office. In the office, we're thinking about the issues (or date nights!) waiting at home.

Third: When we slow down enough to look at and truly be in each moment, **we find that there is PLENTY there to bring us the happiness, contentment and purpose to our lives we are looking for**. (Soak in the warmth of the sun on your face, the chirping birds, the grass between your toes, the snake slithering toward the grass that's between your toes.)

Fourth: When we're fully present in the moment, doing our best to mindfully live in the now, **we let go of any negative or critical judgements of the way things are. Rather, we appreciate all that the moment is, and all that it is *not*.** A great teacher-friend once told me, "All is gift." (For the novice, begin practicing with your son's stinky feet.)

Slowing down and mindfully being present in the *now* of our lives is everywhere today! It's big business, actually. It's yoga, tai chi, the great outdoors, breathing and meditation. It's home and garden magazines, when inviting spaces and relaxing environments are the desired effect. It's fountains and flowers and bird feeders. It can be aromas, soft music, chimes and candles. It's also found in wellness spas, health, fitness and nutrition. It's found in getaways, timeouts and renewing vacations. Even the science behind presence and mindful living techniques has driven contemporary advancements in medical fields like psychology. Being present in the now can also be found rooted in the most enduring religions of the world. And it's AWESOME! Absolutely seismic in its influence.

My learning has taken me down many holes that have no end, and mindfulness has been one of the most exciting. For about a year it seems, while winding down at night, I would listen to one guru or another on YouTube, finding myself trying to be still and alone with my thoughts.

If--like me--peace, purpose, calm, mental & emotional & physical health is what you're after; if more stillness, clarity and balance in the hectic 'race car' madness of life is what you need, enjoy the majestic and ageless wonder that is the Eastern and Western ideology of presence: wakefulness, and living in the now. You can find it all filed neatly under 'mindfulness.'

It works! One of my favorites in the mindfulness genre is Eckhart Tolle and the ideas from his book, *The Power of Now*. In a YouTube video of him as a guest lecturer in front of a large audience he asked those attending to try a dash of meditation with him. He explained they would start at the beginning phase of meditation which he labeled "awareness." He invited them to close their eyes and relax, to breathe gently, and to then gradually become more *aware* of the large auditorium, the atmosphere, the plants and other items on stage, the ceiling, walls, people and energy around them.

He then requested that they move closer into their centers by focusing on their own hands, the feeling or sense of their hands' attachment to their bodies, that they "were" and "are."

The next step was to become conscientious of thoughts as they came into and went out of their minds. He pointed out that it was possible to notice a thought not only separate from other thoughts, but separate from their living and breathing selves, (as a leaf floating down a babbling brook--said another of my favorites at a different time) and he invited them to stand apart from that and other thoughts. They were just to acknowledge the thought, possibly describe it and then let it go, waiting for the next to come.

Lastly, he asked them to notice the space that existed between these thoughts that were coming and going. He asked if they could detect the place where no views were, where no thought was, and yet, a place existed all the same. In the tranquil setting he had masterfully created, with the audience focusing on those spaces that exist between their thoughts, he gently explained… (*Read this next line slowly, with a whisper.*) "That place… is YOU."

And Mr. Tolle would add, I'm sure, (*with a whisper*), "That place is you in the absolute NOW! Just you--with you. As present as you can be."

Whoa! (*Come back gently. Slowly. Inhale. Exhale.*)

The concept of being present is a pillar! Presence is massive in size and enormous in its effects on the universe, just standing there in all of its theoretical colossalness. (Okay editor--how much will that word cost?)

Now--imagine THAT Titan squeezed into the Hadron Collider!

But colliding with what, you ask?

Stay with me!

Man... Mindfulness Missed It

It's pretty much common knowledge that Einstein wasn't a fan of hard butter for his toast. It's *also* common knowledge that he missed a big opportunity with one of his equations. And that's putting it lightly! Had he first trusted his own brilliantly accurate math in his general theory of relativity, instead of doubting himself due to the

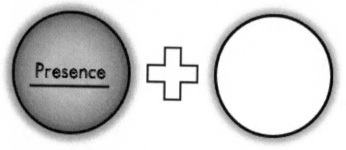

nutty implications it led to, he would've gotten credit for confirming mathematically that the universe is expanding! Instead, he rewrote his equation with an added variable to make the universe remain stagnant and still. (Today, lucky Edwin Hubble receives the credit.)

And that's not all. Without his oopsie, Einstein would have also been given significant acclaim for showing that the idea that everything starting from some infinite point at the beginning of it all--and then exploded outward--was good on paper!

Snap! He admits it was the worst blunder of his career. Many today can casually recall the name he chose for his slightly superstardom-tempering variable: The Cosmological Constant.

Guess what? Mindfulness has missed something too. I know it's hard even to imagine, but for as impressive as mindfulness is, it could have been even *bigger*, even *more* profound, and even had a *greater* impact on the universe and everyone in it! (Aliens too!)

Was it purely an Einsteinian oversight? Maybe it's because mindfulness intentionally, deliberately, (mindfully?) chose to limit its scope.

But for whatever reason, had Western and Eastern philosophy added this amazing, yet missing, 'chocolate' to their titanic 'peanut butter' of <u>Presence</u>, Quintessentialism would be a household (cottage-hold, tent-hold, cave-hold) name!

I guess it's up to me then, to join the one with the other, and to push the button on this Hadron supercollider myself. What an honor! Little ol' me.

. . . .

"My distinguished colleagues and particle accelerator worker people friends, please put <u>Presence</u> in the tunnel-ejection-mechanism-chamber-compartment and prepare to be amazed!"

"Yes, sir! But what will it be smashing into sir? I mean, what goes into the other compartment, sir?"

"What!? You haven't read my book?"

[Cut to black as Mike throws his clipboard.]

A Safety Harness for Mother Teresa

20 years after Mother Teresa organized her Congregation of the Missionaries of Charity in Calcutta, India, a reporter[3] from the BBC was sent to interview her. She'd quietly and unassumingly made a name for herself while helping the destitute in that city, and the world was taking notice.

Interestingly, the reporter came back with a comment that also put HIM on the map! After seeing and feeling of the overwhelming need for help in Calcutta, that included countless, endless poverty, sickness, hunger, and disease in every direction, he printed; "Statistically speaking, what she achieves is little, or even negligible." He felt that the difference she was making was so insignificant that it was hardly worth the trouble.

Mother Teresa believed differently, and her life was a towering monument to that belief! She LIVED the "story of the starfish" as much as anyone of us could. (Do you remember that story? A boy on the beach throwing stranded starfish back into the ocean? A man approaches and says to the boy, "Don't you see the thousands of starfish on this never-ending beach? What possible difference can you make?" The boy picks up another starfish, and after throwing it

---

[3] M. Muggeridge, *Something Beautiful for God: Mother Teresa of Calcutta* (London: Collins, 1971). See also https://speeches.byu.edu/talks/j-michael-hunter small-things; adapted from The Star Thrower, L. Eiseley

back into the ocean says to the man, "It makes a difference to that one.")

No matter the opposing odds, inordinate numbers, staggering statistics, "the insignificant scale by comparison with the need," (to further quote the reporter) Mother Teresa knew that "it made a difference to *that* one" as she helped a starfish back into the ocean, over and over and over again. The reporter suggested institutionalized programs and saw massive government involvement as the only significant way to help. In response to the reporter, Mother Teresa said, "Welfare is for a purpose… love is for a *person*."

A hundred years before this dedicated nun gave her life in the service of others, Charles Dickens gave voice to her philosophy through the first ghost of *The Christmas Carol*. Jacob Marley came to Scrooge from the dead! He visited him as a spirit in chains, bound by his poor choices in life. He wanted to warn and teach his friend about the starfish story--about what was most important. Scrooge couldn't understand what Jacob regretted. He said to him, "But you were always a good man of business, Jacob."

"Business!" says Jacob, "Mankind was my business. The common welfare was my business; charity, mercy, forbearance, and benevolence were, all, my business. The dealings of my trade were but a drop of water in the . . . ocean of my business!"

Even the great Albert Einstein, literally the face that first appears online when searching for the word 'genius,' honored as TIME Magazine's Person of the (20th) Century, said in a letter to his young daughter Lieserl,

"When I proposed the theory of relativity, very few understood me, and what I will reveal now to transmit to mankind will also collide with the misunderstanding and prejudice in the world.

I ask you to guard the letters as long as necessary, years, decades, until society is advanced enough to accept what I will explain below.

There is an extremely powerful force that, so far, science has not found a formal explanation to. It is a force that includes and governs all others, and is even behind any phenomenon operating in the universe and has not yet been identified by us. This universal force is LOVE.

...This force explains everything and gives meaning to life. This is the variable that we have ignored for too long, maybe because we are afraid of love because it is the only energy in the universe that man has not learned to drive at will.

...When we learn to give and receive this universal energy, dear Lieserl, we will have affirmed that love conquers all, is able to transcend everything and anything, because love is the quintessence *of life."*[4]

Like the towering pillar of <u>Presence</u> in our universe, there also exists a second tower of equal or greater footing and of equal or greater height that has also survived from the beginning. We can't ignore it, nor pretend it isn't there, nor deny it hasn't been talked about, sung about, written about and experienced individually in numbers only comparable to grains of sand on the seashore. This second pillar is <u>Humanity</u>. This is the pillar of kindness, compassion, of universal brotherhood and sisterhood, of starfish and of concern for the fellow travelers we live with and work with and interact with throughout our everyday journey on the trail of life.

. . . .

"Sir, I'm not sure it's a good idea to strap Mother Teresa into the Hadron Collider, it's never been done before, and we just can't take the risk, sir!"

"Never tell me the risks, collider installer guy! I laugh in the face of risks! I'm here to take risks NO ONE has risked before! My cape

---

[4] https://monoset.com/blogs/journal/a-letter-from-albert-einstein-to-his-daughter-on-the-universal-force-of-love

says, 'MR. RISK!' But yeah, I do agree with you, bro, she's such a nice lady and a little frail. How 'bout a picture? Do we have a picture of her we can use? And can you throw in a starfish? Oh, and some heart-shaped candies?"

"Picture of Mother Teresa, one starfish and heart-shaped candies to be strapped in, sir!"

"Excellent! Finally, we'll see--once and for all--what happens when the indomitable concepts of <u>Presence</u> *and* <u>Humanity</u> come crashing into one! Put on your safety glasses and buckle up world! Quintessentialism and its accompanying fireworks are about to be BORN!"

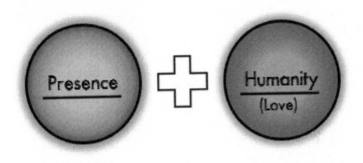

"That is SO Awesome!!"

"So, what happened!?"

"Let me tell you, it was incredible! First, there was this rumbling sound from both tunnel ejection capsules in the Hadron Collider, and it was shaking everything around them! My safety glasses were jiggling off, and the whole place was blurry 'cuz of all the bouncing.

And then, this smoke started billowing out in these giant, white plumes of crazy-cool cotton candy clouds. Just like in the movie *Apollo 13!*"

"No way!? Seriously? That is SO awesome!"

"I know. And then there was this sudden and total SILENCE everywhere as the capsules blasted into light speed. Kinda like in *The Last Jedi* when that spaceship cuts the giant one in half while it's jumping into hyperspace, and you see the explosion and debris flying everywhere, but no sound at all."

"No way!? Are you kidding me? That is SO awesome!"

"I know. And then it was like everyone was holding their breath in complete silence, waiting for an indication of what had happened, ya know, 'cuz we knew that <u>Presence</u> had smashed into <u>Humanity</u>! Everyone's looking around at each other, but nobody's talking. And then there's this... 'beep, beep, beep' sound on a computer screen and that's all you can hear. Kinda like... dang! What's a movie where it's all quiet, and then there's a beeping sound and stuff?

"Oh yeah, I get you. Which movie IS that? Hmmm. Rats! I don't know man, but dang! That is SO awesome!"

"I know. And then we all went over and looked at what was beeping on the screen, and guess what? The computer started sparking and shooting fireworks everywhere because of the magnitude of what had just happened! It's like the computer couldn't even take it! And then guess what? ALL the computers in the whole room began shooting off sparks too--one after another, up and down the rows. And then the ceiling lights went out 'cuz they start sparking too and it was exactly like in *The Natural*, ya know, when Robert Redford hits that World Series home run by blasting the baseball into those giant stadium lights? And then fireworks started spraying all over the field, and the players are all jumping around home plate in the dark and hugging and there are sparkling lights on them too."

"NO WAY! You've got to be kidding me!? That is SO awesome!"

"I know."

"So, what was on the computer screen, that was beeping!?"

"Are you ready?"

"Uh... YAH!"

"It was a graphic organizer, dude!"

"Holy mental map Batman! Are you crazy kidding me!? A graphic organizer!? That is SO awesome!"

"I know. It had one circle labeled '<u>Presence</u>' combining with another circle labeled '<u>Humanity</u>' with 'Love' in parentheses and where the two came together, there was a new shape with writing inside!"

"Get out of here! That is SO awesome! So... what was the shape? What did it say?"

"Sorry man, gotta run!"

"Uh... dude? [*sustained befuddlement with prolonged confusion and silence. Some sporadic blinking.*]

...That was NOT awesome dude!"

Love in the Now!

Scene: A million cameras are flashing all over a press room. Countless reporters are crammed around a blue-draped table and microphones, and cell phones are fighting for space on top. Mike Forsyth is sitting behind the desk, but in front of a white backdrop with his Q logo all over it. He takes a sip of water from his bottle. The cameras go wild. Flashes pop everywhere. Mike squints and holds up his hand to shade his eyes.

Reporter #1: "Mr. Forsyth, Mr. Forsyth! What can we learn from your revolutionizing discovery today, after successfully colliding <u>Presence</u> with <u>Humanity</u> in the CERN Hadron Super Collider?"

Mike: "Great to see you, Jan. Well, we learn *what counts most* in the whole Universe: that's what we learn! We get our first look at Quintessentialism, which is absolutely gorgeous, along with some long-awaited clarity around the END and WHY to life! Super exciting!"

Reporter #2: "Mr. Forsyth, sir! What do you mean exactly? PLEASE explain further! We are dying to know!"

Mike: "Bobby, please call me Mike. How many times do I have to say it? (*Pressroom chuckles.*) These two massive ideologies or concepts that exist in our universe; first that we should live in the present moment as much as we can, and second, that we should be aware of, and lend a hand to those around us, meld into the ultimate axiom for the entire human family. This axiom for all is that we should strive to be fully *present* with *people* as much as possible. Be present with those we're with. Be present with those within our reach. Throw back the starfish along our way. Essentially, to <u>Love</u> in the <u>Now</u>."

Reporter #3: "Amazing news, Mike! Congratulations! Two quick questions: First, I've never seen such excitement about a scientific discovery before. Why do you think this is resonating so quickly with people everywhere? And second, wondering if you could give us a real-world example of this groundbreaking axiom, as you call it. What does it look like, when we're living it?

Mike: "Hey Meredith! Absolutely. Let's start with the first. Discoveries that seem to have been waiting for eons to be made, right there in front of us the entire time, can be especially mind blowing, and that's what's happened here I think. I mean, we've known about Presence forever, and we've known about Humanity's pull within each of us for just as long. We simply never thought to crash these two together to see what we would get. Turns out, it brings a stunningly new perspective to every single minute of our lives!

And to your second question, about a real-world example; there's a million scenarios, but since most of us in this room are at our jobs today, let's start there. Imagine that you're at a table with a colleague, working on a task during lunch. You two had planned earlier in the week that you'd be giving this assignment your complete focus at this moment. It's important, and it's due within hours. You two are striving to be present at work and in life, and you're doing a great job.

"But imagine at that moment someone from your department who unknowingly offended you recently, slides their lunch tray up beside you and is anxious to talk. What do you do? How do you respond?

"Being fully present Now INCLUDES that individual--the person that you're with--and treating and responding to that person with love and humanity. How you engage with this person now sitting beside you is *equally as important* as how you handle the task you're working on."

Reporter #4: "Mike, can you please help me understand a bit more how this melding of two concepts--of loving in the now, as you say--is so revolutionary? Couldn't some argue that it's merely being civil and courteous to the people that come and go?"

Mike: "Thanks for the incredible question! By the way, not sure we've met? What is your name again?"

Reporter #4: "No sir, we haven't. Jackson."

Mike: "Nice to meet you, Jackson. The pleasure's mine! And again, great question! It's revolutionary to me because I postulate that living in the space--where Humanity and Presence come together--is where we are ultimately our very *best selves*. It's, therefore, the goal and the end and the aim of life! Being in this amazing space between Presence and Humanity involves every relationship: our family relationships, our business relationships, and even those brief encounters we make along our way through life.

Reporter #5: "Exciting Mike. So, now that Presence and Humanity have been atomically fused together, forming a new 'Q molecule!?' (*"What whaat?" someone shouts and the room laughs.*) What is the label on that molecule, or the Q section of that graphic organizer?"

Mike: "Thanks, Michelle. It can be labeled several things, *love in the now* is one, *be present with people* is another. I think, however, that it is most accurately expressed as '*Quintessence Personified.*' I say this because, at that precise moment, **where these two pillars come together in your life, the very quintessence of you is occurring: your very best self is happening, or actualizing.**

"Understand that the word quintessence is defined in the dictionary as the purest form or embodiment of a thing. So, essentially, it's you in your purest form, it's you at your very best. It's the quintessential you!"

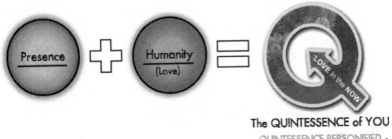

The QUINTESSENCE of YOU
- QUINTESSENCE PERSONIFIED -

Reporter #6: "Mike, with all due respect, you're saying that by being present with those around us, we are at our very best? Can you please elaborate? How does that make us our very best or our quintessential self--if I've said it right?"

Mike: "Superb question! And yes, that's how you say it, Chris. I find that there are three main reasons why *living in the Q* so-to-speak (*Mike is interrupted by some 'woo-hoo's' and more laughter*) is the quintessence of life:

● "First, the **positive impact** one individual can have on another in these quintessential moments is **incalculable**. The effects are so far-reaching--with ripples widening exponentially in all directions-- that the benefit to the one or the countless many simply cannot be measured. One small moment, a smile or even a wink or nod (!) has unlimited potential for profound positive change. You've heard it said that the little things matter most, right? That is especially true in this case. The little things can truly pack a 'Big Bang' punch.

• "Second, this explosive and unlimited potential inherent in every interaction means that **nothing in one's life can supersede it in significance**. That's why, in these Q moments, one reaches their *'Present Potential'*--meaning that they are truly as awesome as they absolutely can be in that instance.

• "Third, by living quintessentially, we also reach our *'Universal Purpose'*--which addresses the commonality between every human being on our planet. It's the great equalizer! No matter the demographics, categories, field descriptors, attributes, or characteristics of one person compared to another, **ALL share an ability to be present with those they are with**. It's the ultimate shared opportunity for every living and breathing individual on Earth. Each one of us, wherever we are, despite all the x and y variables unique to us, can make a positive difference by living quintessentially--by being mindful of humanity, and helping out the starfish within our reach!

Reporter #7: "Awesome, Mike. Thank you! Please tell us more about how this new perspective can benefit people everywhere."

Mike: "Happily, Carlos! How is the baby doing?"

Carlos: "Doing great, man. Thanks. And by the way--thanks for the baby stroller. How in the world do you remember things like that!?"

Mike: "Oh, buddy, don't even mention it. For the record, I'm pretty terrible about remembering all of it. It's just that I'm actually writing this book, and can write in anything I want. So! I got you a baby stroller, dude!"

Carlos: "That's hilarious! Well, in that case, the new Red Audi TT you promised never showed up. Been waiting for a while, man. HA!"

Mike: (*Chuckling hard*) "Carlos--excellent idea! It's there now! Text your wife to look out front and send you the pic! Enjoy it, buddy! (*The room gasps collectively, and then breaks out in celebratory applause.*) So, back to the question--how can this new Q perspective benefit people everywhere?

● "First--I think **people often get confused as to what is MOST important in life, what counts most.** This blasted world can confuse us all! For a while there I thought it was Tom Brady and the New England Patriots. (*Crowd erupts in belly laughs.*) Now we know! It's Humanity plus Presence! It's Quintessentialism!

● "Second--I think it's **hard to know what it means to be your very best self and describe what that looks like exactly**. A clear understanding of this can help every individual navigate each moment of their lives with clarity. It gives them a rubric for handling each situation they come across. It can be a guide for making decisions.

● "Third--It's a **huge boost of self-confidence and satisfaction** to us all, when we can count the many ways we've been totally awesome in a day! (*Again, the crowd laughs.*) With this new understanding, we can now truly celebrate each moment we're being Q! We can let go of where we've been and look forward to more of it in the future!

● "Fourth--When we know what it means to be our very best selves--our quintessential selves--then **many of the stresses and worries and craziness of life go away**: they no longer matter like they used to. I know most people would welcome some of that. It slows life down to interactions and one-by-one moments. Life can't become simpler than that.

● "Fifth--**Life suddenly becomes incredibly more meaningful and purposeful, no matter the present conditions you find yourself in**. Any work-life situation for example--your work position, your job description, your status, and no matter the industry (even while home doing laundry) --it is all seen more as the canvas, more as the means and not the end. You realize that your best self truly can happen in all of those places, and because of that, there is purpose and meaning to where you are and what you are doing today--regardless of the circumstances!"

● "Sixth--Finding ourselves in the Q of life, as often as we can, **becomes a motivating reminder to schedule quintessential moments more often into our lives, consistently and regularly!** When we know what's most important, we're more incentivized to fill our lives proactively with opportunities to be present with the most important relationships around us!"

Reporter #8: "Mike, excuse me, but did I just hear you say that your best self can happen while folding laundry?" (*Audience chuckles.*)

Mike: "Jennifer, you got it! And (!) also while asking questions and reporting at a press conference! (*All the reporters look at each other and smile.*) Let me explain. You're folding laundry. Or for those wanting another scenario, imagine you're at the front desk at work. You recognize it's a part of your life right now. It's your canvas. You slow it down, knowing that it's wonderful to be in the moment, smelling the fabrics, straightening your post-it notes, looking out the window, enjoying the room, etc.

● "What if--at that moment--similar to the scenario discussed before, one of your children comes into the room, or a customer walks into the office? Their entrance now becomes a part of your present moment. You address them with humanity, love, and kindness; meet their needs, be attentive, throwback their 'starfish'; and high five yourself for being in the Q as they walk out. Then, you naturally and smoothly go back to what you were doing.

Or...

"The thought crosses your mind to call someone you haven't talked to in a while. You pick up your phone and give them a call. Here you are, enjoying the moment of folding the laundry, or working the front desk, but you're also fully present, responding attentively to the person on the other end of the line. This is absolutely where living in the moment meets humanity, all while arranging someone's shirt on a hanger or entering addresses into a spreadsheet.

Now, let's take it even further...

● "The person on the other end doesn't answer. Does that change the situation? Nope. You leave them a wonderful message and hang up with a smile on your face. Look at you, Quintessentialist! (*Audience laughs.*)

And...

● "What if the person you're thinking about can't even be called? Your very thoughts about that person--which are noble, loving, full of gratitude and appreciation--absolutely count. Positive ripples go outward, and the universe is changed. Presence and Humanity win! Quintessentialism wins! --all while folding clothes, or working the counter.

Reporter #9: "Mike, great talking to you by the way. But what about setting and reaching goals, achievement, production, chasing dreams, hitting quotas, climbing the corporate ladder? Doesn't this devalue all of that?"

Mike: "Love it, Tom! Another great question. So glad you asked! *Not at all! Put it on the record, please*, that developing one's skills, increasing one's capacity, improving one's abilities and opportunities are all incredibly important! Yes, setting goals, reaching for the stars, pulling yourself up from difficult circumstance and having a determination to succeed in your career and in life *is another inarguable pillar in the universe.* Personally, I am doing my best to improve each day. Sheesh, I'm simply trying to be more present with my wife and kids, for crying out loud! (*Audience chuckles.*)

"What I AM saying though, is that being present with the one you are with, and loving in the now--eclipses and surpasses ALL OF IT! It is the overarching process by which all of this is accomplished. Listen to how those who have achieved enduring success speak of the nobility and importance of honoring the '*process*' in whatever they do. That is especially applicable here, with Quintessentialism. The process of being your best in each moment should be our end and aim."

Reporter #10: What have you found to be most difficult about doing this? What's the hardest part about living quintessentially?"

Mike: "Jerry, how do you all keep coming up with such awesome questions!? Thank you! What's hardest is something that I spend many chapters writing about in my book. I also train organizations on this specific challenge, which is: That to be present with those we're with, we have to SEE them correctly. That can be really hard!"

Reporter #11: "Mike, can you explain that further? What do you mean by seeing people correctly?"

Mike: "Excellent, Cory. Thank you. Well, like I said, it does take additional training to really delve into this, but I'll give you a good example right now, which should help. Imagine you're in an auditorium for a business conference, or it could even be a movie theater if you'd like, waiting for things to begin. The person sitting next to you seems extremely busy, focused on what appears to be very important stuff. She is texting profusely and even takes a call, speaking loudly, with you sitting right there. She doesn't say hi to you or even smile. The question now is, how do you SEE her? There are several ways you can see her, but only ONE way to see her in which you or I could be truly PRESENT with her! And if we are not fully present, we can't be our quintessential self. Seeing others the way we need to--to live in the Q--isn't always easy and takes some intentional work on a consistent basis.

"Here's one more. Imagine you're significant other just stormed their butt out of the room and slammed the door. How do you SEE them *now?*" (*Crowd bursts out laughing!*)

Reporter #12: "Man, I personally can't wait to hear more about that! Mike, you're on record for saying that mindfulness has missed something important during its lengthy run. What do you mean?"

Mike: "Absolutely, Natasha! Thanks. I'll start with a question. When you think of mindfulness today, what immediately comes to mind? For me--and I think for most people--the quick associations are of self-awareness; wakefulness to one's own thoughts, feelings and emotions; as well as that of being mindful of the environment around them, all while being in the present moment. There's a focus on the breath and on stillness and on letting go. Meditation techniques--also associated with mindfulness--take place in a peaceful, solitary setting, with little interruption, as another example. There are traditions of seclusion as a way of becoming even more in tune, present, and aware.

Contrastingly, immediate associations with mindfulness don't generally connect us to the people around us, like our neighbor across the street, or the teller at the drive-through window, or our co-worker over the cubicle wall.

"Interestingly, some of the greatest teachers in mindfulness acknowledge the importance of being aware of others. Absolutely! I would even argue that these teachers are *living in the Q* at a very high level. Still, for whatever the reason, the fact remains that mindfulness just hasn't built its reputation on, or branded itself as being equally focused on our connectivity *to the people around us*.

"Allow me a couple supportive examples of this:

Starting with my mindfulness coloring book, (Haha, 'scholarly'--I know!) which I bought at a prominent and nationally recognized shopping center with a large book and magazine section. Again, I offer this as a snapshot of today's generally accepted view on the topic. Inside my coloring book with many quotes and coloring pages, only *one* quote mentions love at all, and it doesn't specify people. In fact, the only quote that even mentions people speaks of them as a *distraction* from being present.

"One more 'coloring quote' to further illustrate my point. I'll leave off the author because I know they absolutely believe in loving people too. I just want to show that people are not mentioned, when easily they could've been.

"Like a child standing in a beautiful park with his eyes shut tight, there's no need to imagine trees, flowers, deer, birds, and sky; we merely need to open our eyes and realize what is already here; who we already are."

"My second example comes from a word cloud that I made, using an independently organized list of twenty definitions for mindfulness,[5] offered by several dictionaries, thought leaders, acclaimed experts and astute organizations. In my mindfulness word cloud, the word "others" appears only once, in the context of not harming ourselves

---

[5] https://positivepsychologyprogram.com/what-is-mindfulness-definition

and others. There is no other reference to people. And the word love was never used.

Maybe mindfulness wanted to remain generally unattached from the large concept of *humanity* to allow other philosophies to do some heavy lifting. I don't know for sure. I simply desire to acknowledge what is, which is(!) that amazing mindfulness has not yet shaped the dialogue around--and brought conversations and strategies about being fully present with *people*--to the forefront. It's had centuries to do so, but it hasn't happened...yet."

Reporter #13: "Mike, don't people often meditate or do Yoga together, in groups? Isn't that being present with those you are with?"

Mike: "Great thought, Jen! Group settings in which many are participating together in mindfulness exercises could absolutely be including the others they're with. And to that degree--and as long as they're seeing people accurately--they are all most certainly *living in the Q!* Let's call that a Q-Party! (Or is that Zumba?)

"Those experiences, however, are collectively intentional. The environment is more controlled and filled with like-minded individuals that share a common end. There isn't really a focus on achieving presence with the person who is constantly annoying them, or that they are currently in a fight with, or are standing in front of in line, at an amusement park, like Quintessentialism does.

"Additionally, in many cases, showing up to Yoga or another mindfulness activity, and then actually chatting with another individual at the class is left completely up to you. There typically isn't much encouragement from instructors for participants to think about, be aware of, or even get to know each other. It can be a very solitary or individualized experience. Other types of group classes are often more interactive, but it's *still* in your court to reach out to those you're with."

Reporter #14: "Mike, everyone here wants to know why you're so dang awesome!"

Mike: "Johnny G! Enough with that bro! I'm only as awesome as you all! And that's the truth. Now--how 'bout we get into this ice cream I brought for everyone!"

Scene: Mike reaches under the desk and pulls out tubs of the best kind of ice cream ever! The cameras and flashes go NUTS! Everybody starts laughing and high-fiving and whooping and hollering gleefully! Music then begins thumping in the background. People start dancing; reporters pass out bowls and spoons and ask each other how they're doing. Mike has a huge smile on his face as he throws on his favorite '70's shirt and the coolest wig you've ever seen. The DJ and turntable come out, Mike's shades go on and the disco ball comes down. Fade to black.

CHAPTER 3
The Quintessential Message in a Bottle!

Bring Back Stompers!

Bring back, Stompers! I mean, why this hasn't happened in the 21st century, I have no idea! They were clearly the coolest toy from the 80's. Maybe the coolest toy ever invented, and now you can hardly find them online. With all the throwback stuff coming out these days, this is an absolute no-brainer.

Imagine a totally tough looking 4x4 just a bit bigger than a matchbox car, with big 'ol wheels rockin' massive tread and room under the truck body's casing for one AA battery. These things would climb over anything when you turned them on. Pencils, rocks, babies-- you name it! They even came with exchangeable soft wheels for indoor use and harder rubber wheels for nature's tough terrain. Who didn't love setting up obstacle courses for these little crawlers to obliterate? Stompers in our Christmas stockings, is what I say!

And just like the coolest toy that needs a rebirth, one of the coolest and most insightful philosophers of our modern age needs a resurgence as well. But unlike Stompers, this is something I can absolutely do something about. I'm taking matters into my own hands world!

Allow me to reintroduce you--modern age--to the individual who makes living quintessentially with all people a REAL possibility, and NOT mere wishful thinking!

A Message in a Bottle

Martin Buber (*1898--1965*) was a philosopher--like Immanuel Kant--who believed that finding meaning and purpose to life was found outside of oneself (as one looked outward to his or her surroundings) and promoted meaningful connection to what existed there. Born in Austria (and dying 67 years later in Jerusalem), Martin made a contribution to the world--in several significant ways--unmatched by any other philosopher. The implications of his insight open the door to quintessential opportunities for every person, every day of their lives!

This understanding is described in his life's opus, *I and You*, (Or *I and Thou* in a different translation.) Written just over a century ago, his words come to us like a message in a bottle--a message for a future time--when we'd find it once again.

A message that's practically unreadable!! Martin--seriously? Who did you expect to understand this, dude!? Could you have thought to write and shove a copy of *Me and You for Grade Schoolers* in the bottle while you were at it? We are not all doctors in philosophy, man. Just a tip there, pal. Sheesh--even the gentleman that translated your German into English said your book was truly "untranslatable"!

That being said: I'm no Aristotle, but let me see if I can help.

Martin says that we see others in only two ways. The first is as an *object* or a thing. He calls seeing people this way as viewing them as "ITs," which makes sense when we understand that 'IT' is the pronoun we use to identify non-living things. 'ITs' can be obstacles in our way, for example, preventing us from getting what we want. 'ITs' can also be vehicles used as a means to move us further along the path we're trying to pursue, to further our ends. Another way of seeing people as 'ITs' occurs when we don't notice them, or pay the smallest attention to them, because they have nothing to do with our plans or direction. They are seemingly irrelevant to us, in every sense.

Think of it! Throughout the course of a single day, we may have hundreds or even thousands of interactions with other human beings. And yet, many of these interactions (most? all?) are viewed through our distorted lenses portraying them as objects, obstacles, vehicles, or as being irrelevant!

"Out of my way please--I'm kind of important, and my ice cream is melting."

"Can you believe what he said about me? I'm surprised he even knew the word 'superficial'! By the way, what does that mean?"

"I need you in here NOW! And stop laughing! Oh, you think seeing my tie stuck in the shredder is funny, do you!? Keep it up and you're fired the moment I'm free. Uh...fired *after* you do payroll I mean! Actually, fired right after you find and train your replacement!"

"I'm sorry, I think I've forgotten your name for like the twentieth time. OH! Excuse me! I accidentally confused you with someone else that I don't actually know. So, what's *your* name? Oh, I've asked you that already too? Twenty times already?"

Buber's Brilliance!

As cool as Buber's 'IT' INsight IS, however, it's not the explosive 'a-ha' that's coming! Ready? Martin explains that seeing a person as an 'IT' actually says MORE about the *person seeing,* (or grammatically speaking, the *subject*) than it does about the person being seen (the *direct object*). This is because how you see others, is a manifestation of who <u>you</u> are. More simply, you are as you see others.

Martin creates his own language of sorts to describe this interrelationship between ourselves and the perceived objects around us. He puts an 'I' in front of the 'IT' and connects them both with a hyphen, making it one word. I-IT is a descriptive word, a label, name, or state of being for anyone viewing another as a thing.

Just when you thought an insight couldn't get cooler than this last one--which was cooler than the first one--guess what? Have I got an *even cooler* insight for you! This latest insight's coolness begins when further dots are connected, and we begin to insightfully see what we and others are like as I-IT people!

Let me clarify this. We all know what it's like to be standing behind someone taking forever in the checkout line. We're in a hurry, and somehow, we got behind the wrong person! Of course, they have a coupon somewhere they can't find. And now their debit card is being temperamental. And yep, the communication is difficult. Good grief!

"Let's GO already! The line is backing up," you say to yourself.
"Have your coupons together beforehand, for crying out loud,
instead of making the rest of us pay for your poor preparation."

What words could we use to describe ourselves, or others in that I-
IT frame of mind? I'll list a few for starters:

annoyed	upset	angry	selfish	self-centered
uncaring	irked	cross	testy	unsympathetic
egocentric	prickly	cranky	perturbed	self-absorbed
grumpy	touchy	peeved	egotistical	exasperated
uncaring	irked	cross	testy	grumpy

Can you believe it!? All of those negative attributes so accurately
describe us when we're in our I-IT world, seeing another person as
an obstacle in our way. And it can happen so quickly, so
unexpectedly. And for many of us, so consistently, so regularly.

The Me-Zone

What each of these words describe, is someone very much thinking
and concerned about themselves. Each describe someone
exclusively focused on their interests. Their life, when feeling this
way revolves around their plans, their agenda, their timing, and their
world. It's looking inward and not outward. I call it the "Me-
Zone," and when we're in it we see others as objects; obstacles in
our way or vehicles to be used to further our ends.

And it's easy to tell when we're in the Me-Zone too, because we
feel and experience the negativity associated with each adjective.
Those words accurately describe us, and the feelings connected with
those words are a part of us as well.

And when I use the word negativity to describe how these words feel, that might be putting it lightly! Yes, those feelings are more than just negative, they're loathsome at worst and naggingly unpleasant at best. We actually hate being in the Me-Zone. Of course, we're not happy there. Who's happy barking, snapping, bossing others, putting people down, and being angry and insecure all the time? No one.

And those around us sure aren't happy either. Ever hugged a porcupine? There's a reason the Grinch lives alone! People influenced by our scratchy and icy Me-Zone way of being become even more put-off by the mumbling and grumbling and self-centered comments. Dark ripples dampen more and more moods of more and more people. They see *US* as obstacles. Resentment begets more resentment. Dork begets more dorkiness. "I can't believe you did that," begets "I can't believe YOU did that, Mr. Prickly!" No one's *really* listening to or caring about our life's ups and downs. They're not hugging us when we leave. They're glad when we're gone. No holiday or birthday cards for us. No parties, no smiles, no thank-yous.

Conclusion: I-IT people are self-absorbed and miserable. Some live there, but any time spent in the Me-Zone equates to a hard, heavy, defensive, insecure and lonely way of living and being.

And it's the same with seeing others as vehicles too. Imagine noticing someone on campus that you really don't see yourself being friends with, but they just happen to be in one of your classes, and have the answers to the test that you didn't study for.

"Hey, handsome! How's it going?" you ask as you sit down across from him in the student lounge, working your smile just so. "It's been forever, huh? Did you go to the game? Anything fun after?

We should totally hang out at the next one! For sure! I've wanted to do something with you forever, but it just gets so busy, yeah know. Liking our class lately? Oh my gosh! I think this test is gonna kill me!"

fake	deceptive	two-faced	insincere	manipulative
crafty	disingenuous	artificial	phony	counterfeit
sly	cunning	duplicitous	false	conniving

If, as they say, "beauty is as beauty does" --that's *ugly!*

And along with being aloof, uncaring, thoughtless, indifferent, blasé, unconcerned, emotionless, distant, remote, stuffy, unnoticing and self-absorbed when we see others as *irrelevant*, allow me to share one more example. (Try to guess which way you're seeing another in this particular Me-Zone situation.)

A new hire at work seems to be brilliant, catching on quickly and liked by your manager. Is it possible that you could be, or ever have been:

insecure	threatened	defensive	anxious	apprehensive
afraid	unconfident	unsure	guarded	vengeful
cold	protective	hesitant	malicious	unforgiving
bitter	untrusting	hurtful	vindictive	incredulous
hostile	concerned	spiteful	mean	vulnerable

All of this negativity because of I-IT and Me-Zone perceptions! And to make matters worse--if it's even possible at this point--these perceptions are almost always false and inaccurate. (I really wanted to leave out the word 'almost' right then, but I'll save that for another page.)   These blurred and faulty perceptions are of our own doing! Our glasses are smudged.

Oh, what to do!?

Wait a second! Didn't Martin say there was another way of seeing people? Please tell me this is thus!

CHAPTER 4
Another Way of Seeing (Quintessentially!)

'Cuz this Me-Zone thing Ain't Workin'!

I'd like to explain this next way of seeing others through a story:
About ten years ago I was working in an office, responsible for
orchestrating live and online continuing education trainings for
mortgage brokers. Each year mortgage brokers need a certain
number of continuing education credits, and we made that happen
for many.

On this particular day, and at this specific time I was extremely
anxious about finishing up something that had a hard deadline. I was
frantically working away, completely engulfed in what I was doing,
hoping that time would be my friend as I kept looking up at the
clock in nervous anticipation.

The phone on my desk started to ring, and I let it go for a while.
Wondering who it might be, and allowing curiosity to get the best of
me, I grabbed the phone, and immediately realized what a huge
mistake I had made!

This was no important call. It was a customer service issue, and I
absolutely had no time for it. To make it worse, the gentleman on
the other end spoke with a very difficult to understand accent. I had
to strain to hear him. I shook my head, rolled my eyes, scooted the
phone under my chin and held it against my shoulder. Back to work
for me! My plan was to listen enough to let him think we'd help
him eventually, and hopefully get him off the phone as quickly as
possible. My deadline couldn't wait. Clickety-clack, my fingers
went with the occasional "uh-huh" and "okay" and "hmmm" to let

him know I was still there. I was as I-IT and in the Me-Zone in that moment as one could be. Feel free to use any of the negative adjectives listed above to describe me. This 'thing' on the other line was in my way. Move over buddy. Stuff to do.

Not sure how long this continued, but I think a good angel was jumping up and down on my shoulder for quite some time, pulling on my earlobe and screaming at me to listen for a minute. Truly, I take no credit for the rest of this story.

What did happen, however, is that I caught a word despite all of my efforts to focus on what I deemed was more important--my work. The word was "hospital." For some reason, I paused. And then I replied to the voice on the other end of the line.

"Excuse me. Can you go back? Did I just hear you say something about a hospital?"

"Yes, that is what I've been trying to tell you!" he said. "I am calling you from a hospital bed. I am here now with tubes running in and out of me, and machines are everywhere. I'm extremely sick. Even so, I have to finish my online course right away and I can't log in. If I don't work on this now, my license will expire, and I will no longer be able to provide a living for my family."

... *Crickets* ...

What happened next is beyond my ability to fully explain, but in an instant, guess what? Nothing else mattered anymore, except helping this man, in his dire situation.

It's the craziest thing. Truly, I'll repeat it for emphasis: nothing on my desk mattered anymore. I mean it. It's like it vanished away. The deadline, the clock, the anxiousness, and stress--it was all gone.

It was nowhere to be found. ALL that was left was me wanting to do everything I could to help this individual who needed me in this moment.

And I helped him. And I was genuinely happy to do it! Ten years later, I can't remember the names of any of our clients from that company now. Except his. His name is Bipen Patell. He was calling me from Texas, and if you're out there somewhere reading this buddy, whassup!?

In mere seconds, I had completely changed. No pretending, no efforting, but real change, foundational, fundamental core change-- through and through. In a snap, I went from being a self-absorbed me-me-me I-IT guy to seeing someone in a way that Martin Buber describes as I-THOU or I-YOU.

I saw Bipen, NOT as a thing, not as an object or as an IT, but as a remarkable individual, in all of his humanity. He had hopes and dreams like me. He had challenges, headaches and pain like me. He was a person to me now. He was real to me now.

"When understanding arises, compassion is born." -Thich Nhat Hanh

"There are two kinds of people in the world; those you love, and those you don't know." -Anonymous

Martin describes seeing people this way phenomenally well. He says that when we see another as a YOU, they are beyond our ability to accurately define. They cannot be categorized, or plotted anywhere on a graph. They are more than any words could ever describe. They are more than any age, gender, size, demographic, position, nationality, height or any other category or field that we could sort them by. They are more than the clothes they wear, the color of their skin, the language they speak. They are more than any title or waist size, more than their current circumstances, more than who they are today, or tomorrow, or yesterday, or years and years ago, or years and years from now. We sense that it is impossible for us to fully know everything about them. They are gloriously complex and infinite. Because of this, we respectfully "stand in relation" to them, says Buber. We honor them, and do so with a title of respect that one version of his book translates into 'thou.'

Do you want to hear it in Martin's words? Try this:

"The human being to whom I say 'You', I do not experience. But I *stand in relation to him*, in the sacred basic word. ...Only as things cease to be 'our You' and become 'our It' do they become subject to coordination... describable, analyzable, classifiable... an aggregate of qualities... The 'You' knows no system of coordinates." (*italics added*)

The We-Zone

And possibly the greatest insight of all from Buber is this: when we see others this way, *we* are changed!

No longer are we a long list of negatives, but just the opposite! Check these words out, describing you and me when we're in an I-YOU place with those around us. The We-Zone! The Q Zone!

patient	tolerant	forgiving	cooperative	affectionate
kind	merciful	sensitive	approachable	neighborly
caring	humane	friendly	benevolent	accommodating
gentle	attentive	abundant	sympathetic	thoughtful
loving	helpful	gracious	compassionate	forbearing
warm	tender	accepting	understanding	_present_

Mind-blowing, huh? And it all happens, NOT because others change, but because *we see others differently!* And guess what else!? People in the We-Zone are... you guessed it: happy, joyful, fulfilled, satisfied, cheerful, glowing, peaceful, still, gratified, contented, merry, glad, untroubled, delighted, excited, elated, exuberant and on and on.

Consider the profound truth in all of this: we can be positively and amazingly free from so many (even all) negative attributes that are so heavy to bear, without any obligations for or expectations of others to change. We are in complete control. We are totally free. We determine how often we are residing in our I-ITness and how often we're not.

A few pages ago, I'm sure somebody out there began wondering about the seeming inevitability of seeing another as a vehicle during business transactions. "Aren't we using people to further our ends in those situations?" you may ask. Famous German philosopher Immanuel Kant had something to say about this!

*"Act in such a way that you treat humanity... never **merely** as a means to an end, but always at the same time as an end." -Immanuel Kant (emphasis added)*

In every transaction in which both or all parties are willing participants, the goal and end is that ALL individuals gain from the exchange, and walk away happier and wealthier than they were before. Free market exchange *should* be a win-win! And in those cases, people are indeed seen as YOUs, as ends in and of themselves, and not merely as a vehicle, to be used for another's exclusive self-interest.

There are two additional insights that Martin Buber provides in his book *I and Thou* that are profoundly related to Quintessentialism. These insights also give deeper meaning to my terminology, the We-Zone, and even the Q-Zone. (Anyone works!)

You Complete Me

The first key insight by Buber is that **without other people, we CANNOT be our very best selves**, we cannot be complete, whole, or the measure of ourselves in its fullness. We need others in order for us to be fully expressive in our potential as humans. Here it is in his own words:

"The basic word I-You can be spoken only with one's whole being... I require a You to become; becoming I, I say You."

It is this connectedness that makes us who we are. It is this connectedness that allows us to be quintessential!
The word "Ubuntu" originates from Africa and anciently meant "I am because we are." A beautiful phrase, and affirms in part what Buber is expressing.

However, I'd like to take it even one step further if I may, and I believe Mr. Buber would agree. (And maybe we can pull it out of his sentence above if we look closely.) It's not just that we're all connected to the great human family like roots and branches from the same single tree, although that's absolutely an eloquent thought! And it's not just that we *are*, because of those that raised us, taught us, influenced us and were there for us throughout our lives. That too is powerful, no doubt. Both ideas are necessary. We wouldn't exist at all, or exist *as* we are, any other way.

But I see it as even more personal and intimate than that. For you and I to reach our full potential in the moment, to be our very best, we even *need* the person that we say hi to, as they walk past us on the street. We need the person we wave to as we turn the corner in our car. For us to be our quintessential selves, we need the individual we're angry with in the office, we need the child that pulls our face toward theirs with their chubby hands, we need the man or woman that's crying for us to listen, we need the attendant at the convenience store, we need the student or coworker that tries our patience. Yes, the quintessence of you and me blossoms in our togetherness **with those along our path, and with those within our reach**.

"Love does not cling to an I as if the You were merely its... object: (Love does not exist in I-IT) it is between I and You. For those who stand in [I-YOU] and behold in [I-YOU], ...[they] emerge from their entanglement in busy-ness; ...and now [they] can act, help, heal, educate, raise, redeem. Love is a responsibility of an I for a You." -Martin Buber

"Welfare is for a purpose... love is for a person." -Mother Teresa

Present with (a) YOU

The second insight by Martin Buber, is as equally essential to the existence of Quintessentialism. The first is saying, "You can't be your best without the others you're with," and now, the second is saying, "You cannot be **fully present, in the moment, living in the now**, without seeing others in the I-YOU, We-Zone way!" Check out this quote:

"The present...exists only insofar as...encounter, and relation exist. Only as the You becomes present does presence come into being." -Martin Buber

Okay, here's my translation: (Dang you, Buber!) Being fully present exists *within* relationships. Only when the I-You emerges between you and another person does your being fully present with them occur. (Hey, not bad!)

To make sense of this profound insight, I think about my young son who I often put to bed at night. (As I've done with my other children before him.) Unfortunately, I must admit that this can often be an I-IT affair. I'm tired, it's been a long day. He's already been on my nerves once tonight and I'm interested in going back downstairs to do my thing, watch my game or anything really, besides tuck him in and read a story. In that moment, I am not fully present with my son. Rather, I am seeing him as an obstacle in my way, and as long as I continue to see him as an obstacle, I won't be, nor can I be *present* with him. I'll go through the motions, turn the pages, kiss him goodnight, head back down stairs, and will have missed out on a more deeply meaningful moment together, where father and son magically engage in quality time; connecting, sharing, interacting and truly being present with each other.

How often are we *with* people, but not fully *present* with them? For me, the answer is a scary one.

Remember the two colleagues working busily on a task during lunch? They are considerately present with each other and focused on the task at hand, which is wonderful, but how they see the interruption sliding up beside them (the one from whom a recent offense had been taken) will determine if they can remain fully present by... *being present with the ones they're with.* If she's an obstacle to them, it's lost. If she's real to them, they'll nail another quintessential moment with their colleague. They'll be their best selves before lunch!

Fused Together

It was fun imagining the pillar of <u>Humanity</u> and our picture of Mother Teresa strapped in tight inside the CERN Hadron Collider, thinking about what could happen when it smashed into <u>Presence</u> at light speed. All this "Quantum Quintessentialism" gets the imagination flowing.

There are, however, two things, both incredibly real, that happen when we find ourselves *living in the Q.* It's at this point in our discussion that metaphor comes to its end and the fusing of these two concepts in actuality begins.

As we've been taught by Martin and explored at length together, only when we love (Humanity) in the now, (Presence) are we I-YOU, in the We-Zone and living quintessentially. Read this next paragraph slowly, because I don't know how else to emphasize this first point deservedly enough. Ready?

Presence and Humanity, truly, literally, fuse together: like when forces are so strong that atoms become one and super energy is released; 'love' and 'now' also become one, with equally powerful energy radiating outward.
The *time* that this happens is when you're *in the Q,* the <u>*place*</u> where this happens is <u>*inside your heart*</u>.

. . . .

The second point, equally as real, and equally as wonderful (please read it equally as slowly) is as follows:

Not only do Love and Now fuse together in our hearts when we're in the Q, but like two atoms that bond together to form an element, **your heart also bonds with the person you're with**. You become a bonded, connected pair. A pair that work as one!

Bonded in a Blink

I was in a Me-Zone mood. Grumpy. I remember I was home, and old enough then to tear off on my bike and get some quick distance between me and a bad day. I can't remember exactly what had me up and outta there so quickly, but I bet it was a lot of self-absorbed aggravation that came to a tipping point. I was off!

I was peddling to my friend's house exactly one mile away, as it turns out, (thanks, Google maps!) and every downward push of my leg released some ornery fumes of some sort. Every second I coasted was a chance to complain about something else. I weaved across the busy street, jumped the curb and was on a clear sidewalk straightaway for a good block or two. A large fenced orchard was on my left. My storm cloud was following me.

Up ahead was someone walking my direction. I had to make sure I passed her on the left, and when I did, I glanced at her quickly, to see who would be instantly eating my dust. She smiled at me.

I had never seen her before, but I had *heard* about her before. I think it was my mom who told the story about a girl and her siblings that lived somewhere within our community of Orem, Utah. Many years earlier, her mother, who had been suffering from a mental illness, tragically tried burning the house down with her children inside. I know that at least one of the girls survived. She had a scarred face from the fire.

And she smiled at me.

To the girl who walked past me that day, I don't know your name, or where you are, or anything more about you. But you need to be in my book, in order that somehow, some way, some day, I may be able to thank you for changing my mood instantly. I was a better person in the milliseconds following our brief exchange. I am a better person writing about you now. Your smile has had a lasting impact on me. You are the only evidence needed to show that living quintessentially knows no bounds, or speed limits. And that bonding with another person... can happen with a smile--and in a blink.

Wherever you are--*thank you!*

. . . .

The woman has now been standing at the checkout counter for some time. Having just barely found her coupon in an obscure purse pocket, she can't believe that now her debit card isn't working! The patience of those behind her has worn thin, and she hears a couple sharp comments in a foreign language that only mean one thing, and she understands it. It rattles her. She's getting more flustered and confused and panicky. She isn't at all sure what to do. She doesn't have enough to pay for the medicine with cash. It would be terrible to leave without it. She knows she has the money in her account, it was transferred there that very afternoon. She has now turned in desperation to wishing for a small miracle: that her card can communicate with the machine, just once.

Upon seeing this woman's distress, the individual directly behind her steps close and says to the cashier directly, "Let's go ahead and swipe this one," handing out his card. He smiles to the flustered woman, and when she realizes what has happened, she puts her hands to her eyes. She's overwhelmed with gratitude.

They walk out of the store together and smile one last time before going different directions. Being present with the one, you are with fused together in that moment. The energy is radiant. All else is surpassed. Quintessentialism wins again.

For me, it is an honor to be considered a member of the great human family that includes our world-changing genius: Albert Einstein. He's on my 'Top 5 People to Invite to Dinner' list. I wonder if he wouldn't mind my adding a slight addendum to his quintessential phrase of love:

"The quintessence of life is lov[ing those within your reach.]"

CHAPTER 5
Q--I Need You!

A Rapid Response

"Hello--this is Mike."

"Hi, Mike--this is Carlos from the press conference the other day. Did I catch you at a bad time?"

"Whatsup, Carlos!? Great to hear from you! Not at all--perfect timing, actually. I'm running some class 5 rapids with my family somewhere on the Colorado River, and since they're all focused on surviving right now, let's chat.'"

"Perfect! So, hey--thanks for my sports car, man! It's been so nice, and my wife is happy too."

"Don't mention it!" Mike says as he quickly puts the phone under his chin so he can hold on to two ropes with both hands. "I put it in the book. That's all I did!"

"This imaginary stuff is AWESOME Mike! Well, thanks again. So... two questions really quick." Carlos waits for a reply and doesn't hear anything. "Mike? Mike...?"

"Hey! I'm back! So sorry! My phone bounced down into the raft. It was sliding everywhere! Took just a second to catch that thing. What's your question?"

"Sweet! So... in the press room you were saying that being present with people is when we're absolutely our best self and living quintessentially. Well, I've been thinking. What about people that are doing what they totally love, like performing on the stage or playing their favorite sport. Aren't they their very best *then*?"

"Great question, Carlos! You mentioned a performance first, so let's start there. Imagine a dancer on stage performing beautifully for a packed house. Or maybe it's someone singing a song while playing a guitar in a coffee shop. They're both doing what they love and in that amazing moment life is huge and exciting and wonderful--right?

"Right!" agrees Carlos. "Exactly!"

"Do you think in that moment that these performers are connecting with their audience, fully present with those that came to listen and participate? Playing and giving all they can to those that are there?"

"Absolutely," says Carlos. "Well, at least I would hope so." *Silence on the line.* "Mike? You there...?"

"Sorry, Carlos! Dang rapids! Hit a boulder and the phone bounced out again. Barely caught the thing! My daughter's head saved the day! And you're right--a performer is connecting with their audience! Because here's what we want to remember: **to the degree that any performer**, ballet dancer, juggler, stand-up comedian, you name it, **is living in that special We-Zone place, with a desire to give themselves and their talents fully to the many 'THOU's' sharing the moment with them--they ARE** *living in the Q!*

"Now check this out! Oh wait--hold on one sec..." (You can now hear Mike with the phone to his life jacket, asking his wife a question.) *"Babe. Babe. Can you please grab the little guy?"* as Mike points his chin in junior's direction. *"He's about to fall out…*Alright-- I'm back pal."

"Hey Mike--if now's a bad--"

"Heavens, NO! My kids are scared speechless right now. They're absolutely paralyzed, man. No other conversations are happening right now but ours, Carlos.

"So--what's even MORE amazing, is when the *audience* emotionally connects with the *performers!* The audience is feeling the rush too, as they are connected to those on stage and their amazing gifts and talents and bravery and effort. They cheer! They applaud! In other words--to the degree that an **audience member is living in that special We-Zone place, with a desire to give of themselves to the 'THOU' performing--they are ALSO living quintessentially!**

"It's such an amazing moment, when both audience and performer are connected to each other, appreciating each other, blessed by each other and each one giving the best they have to the other. Performers need an audience just as much as an audience needs performers. It truly is a quintessential moment in every way.

"And it's the same with sports--especially when the team is gelling and the fans are going nuts! You know Carlos--like your frog jumping championship you were telling me about! That is Q to the max! Hold on one secooooond!" (*Mike's voice trails off in a massive crescendo.*)

"Mike!? Mike!? Are you okay!?"

(*Gurgling sound*)

"Carlos--did you hang up? I'm wet, but I'm okay. Fell out for just a second, but everything's alright now. What's your next question?"

"Wow!" exclaims Carlos. "I really can't believe..."

"Don't mention it. With all this horizontal whitewater, my family can't see anything! Happy to hit the next one with you, pal!"

"So... what about that psychological term called 'flow.' Have you heard of it? When you're in the 'Zone' they say, completely engaged in something you love to do and are good at, totally losing track of time, and absolutely clicking on every cylinder. Isn't *that* being at your best?"

"I love it man--great question! I absolutely know what flow is and I agree--being in that moment when you're hyper-focused and losing all sense of space and time is TOTALLY INCREDIBLE! I know a guy that describes skiing that way. And I've been in the flow before while water coloring and even writing this book. Two points here Carlos. First, chapter 9 of my book is all about understanding *yourself* truthfully, in order to be *fully present* with that amazing individual! **When we are in 'the Zone' or experiencing flow, we ARE *living in the Q!*** We are enjoying the moment *with the good-looking person in the mirror!* We like ourselves. We're glad we are who we are. We're pleased with our accomplishments and abilities. We enjoy doing what we're doing AND enjoy the 'THOU' we're doing it with. How neat it is to be there!

"And Carlos, moving on to the next point, here's one I know you can answer. What's *more* incredible than *incredible!?*"

"Incredible *shared?*" Carlos wonders. "Incredible *with* someone?"

"Carlos--two seconds buddy! GRAB MY PADDLE!! *GRAB MY PADDLE!!*" (*Moments pass, and muddled hysteria and then garbled cheers can be heard.*)

"Carlos, I'm back. Uh... (*deciding whether to share*) it's all tears of happiness here, man!

"And Yes... exactly! **Incredible *multiplied*! Incredible *squared*!** I know a family who loves boating. While they're out on the water together, time flies and everything else going on in life is forgotten. Well, guess what? They often take someone they've never met before, someone they've learned has never been on a boat, and may have few opportunities to do so in their future. Flow by the *Q degree!* That kind of stuff is unmeasurable! Unquantifiable!"

"I love it man," says Carlos. "It makes so much sense. Mike--thanks a lot buddy. Thanks for your time and--"

"Carlos! No problem man, but I've got to run! We must've taken a wrong turn!! We're Indiana Jonesin' this thing! We're going over a CLIFF, DUDE!!"

"Mike! Mike!" Carlos screams, "Write in parachutes! Write into your book 'parachutes'!"

"Way ahead of you, buddy! PEACE OUUUT!"

Seeing is *Being* Quintessential

Thanks to Martin Buber, it becomes clear that to truly be present with the endless stream of humanity as they file along through our lives, we must see them truthfully, as a 'THOU.' We need to be in the We-Zone. Otherwise the quintessential equation will fall apart, evaporate away or never germinate in the first place. This is so because the two pillars of <u>Presence</u> and <u>Humanity</u> have been interrupted by our I-IT, Me-Zone perceptions. Only when we get to I-YOU, can we genuinely desire to help and love and care (Humanity) and be completely immersed in the moment (Presence).

It behooves us all, then, to learn the art of being present with others by seeing them correctly! *Seeing* is the key that opens the door to *being* present with those around us, and genuinely loving them too, thus reaching the quintessential sweet spot!

Attack of the Cardboard Cutouts

Taz woke up late, and that was the last thing he needed today! "Why didn't my alarm go off?" he thought to himself. "Was someone playing with my phone?"

Taz was out of bed in a blink, tripping over toys and clothes on the floor and frantically looking in his closet for something clean to wear. It's a good thing his hair was short because there was no time for a shower now!

Down the stairs and into the kitchen he blew like a whirlwind, to find his wife at the sink looking out the window. "Oh! There you are. Can I have your smoothie this morning--right here on the counter? I'm so late!"

As Taz is looked for his keys--while stuffing his bag and waiting for his wife, Violet, to answer--he thought about their argument the night before. It' had been the same thing for who knows how long between them, why couldn't she figure it out!?

"Violet--I'm taking your smoothie because I'm LATE. Can you make another?" he said abruptly and louder, assuming his wife hadn't heard the first time. There was no response. "Violet!" he yelled, before going over to where she was, to really get her attention.

As he touched her shoulder, he went from grumpy to horrified when her body twisted around to face him slightly and then fell backward toward the counter, sliding away to where a pulled-out drawer stopped her fall. She was looking blankly off to the distance and very thin. She was a cardboard cutout!

After a scream that the kids at the bus stop could hear, he stumbled back and rubbed his eyes. "I must be dreaming! I'm not awake!"

But he was awake.

"But I AM awake!" he said out loud, while pinching himself and slapping his face. "I'll figure this out as soon as I can, I promise!"

In a flash, Taz was out the door, tripping over cardboard while doing so. Pulling out of the driveway, he wondered where the twins had been this morning. He always heard them. They had to have been up.

"Out of the street!" he yelled at his windshield, swerving to miss a group of middle-schoolers waiting for the bus. "Those dang kids never learn!" But this time as he swerved, he blew several of them down. He crashed into a garbage can while staring out the rearview. "This can't be possible!" Cardboard cutouts, every one.

The construction crew, the crossing guard, the other drivers in front and behind, even all the students outside the school he was about to enter--flat, corrugated.

Using the key hanging from his lanyard, Taz flew into the lobby to see Mrs. Rose at the front office reception desk. She was smiling at him. "Mrs. Rose! Thank heavens you're real! Something crazy has happened and I need your help!" Mrs. Rose had been at the middle school forever, and Taz believed she should be retired by now. She doesn't have the snap and decisiveness one should have in her role. She gets to Taz' requests only after she's finished with everything else--at least that's how it seemed to Taz.

Fumbling for a sheet of paper in his bag, he said, "Mrs. Rose, I really need your help immediately this time, please! Can you get this copied and in my box for 1st period? I'll have a student come down and get them.

"Mrs. Rose. Mrs. Rose!" But it was no use. As real as she might've seemed only seconds ago, she had now been Han-Soloed--frozen in cardboard carbonite.

"Fine. The kids can read silently first hour," Taz mumbled to himself while whirling down the hall, with papers flying, blowing over cardboard people as he ran.

And then suddenly the whirling stopped... and Taz, now walking softly up to his classroom door, turned around slowly, and slid his back down smoothly to the floor. Defeated. Taz realized 4 yards back that the key to his room was somewhere between his front lawn and the long hallway. It had fallen off his lanyard AGAIN!

(And how many times had he asked Ms. Petunia for a more efficient lanyard!)

Moving his surrendered gaze up from the tile to the cutouts that were either littering the floor or standing throughout the hallway, he saw a few people that he worked with, unmoving in various positions, strewn among the students.

There was Mr. Birch, the science teacher with a smile and a hand raised for a high-five. "Science teachers always get to be the funnest," Taz thought to himself, "whether they actually teach the kids anything or not."

And then there was Ms. Lily, "who can't let go of a grudge, smiling all sweet-like at Mr. Willow, who never liked me from the first day we met," Taz recounted to himself.

And way down the hall was Mrs. Daisy, "who's always good for a laugh at staff meetings" but said to Taz recently that he'd be the perfect teacher to oversee the chess club. "I told her three years ago that I wasn't good at board games!"

"And Ms. Daffodil can't keep a secret and Mr. Cottonwood never used a single one of my ideas for spirit week and Doug Fir took the promotion I wanted…"

And then there's Principal Alstroemeria-Delphinium, who was two dimensional only 10 feet away from his classroom! "Thank every Greek god that she's cardboard right now because she absolutely cannot know I'm running late *and* lost my key in the same morning!"

Taz then turned to the motionless kids, counting all his 'problem students' from the rest he didn't know. He was somewhere between 13 and 38 when he thought he heard some whistling down at the far end of the hall. He stopped and listened to make sure he wasn't mistaken. Indeed, it was real! Someone was walking his way, whistling and swinging a lanyard around her finger.

Ten echoing footsteps later he knew who it was! Weaving in and out of flat statues was Ms. Bird of Paradise--his one friend these days! She was new to the area this year and had somehow gotten on his good side early. It might've been the way she joked back at his sarcasm. Or that she non-judgmentally helped him with his filing. Maybe it was her story about living in 9 foster homes before graduating, but whatever the reason, he sure was happy to see her! (But not happy enough to run toward her.) "Be cool, be cool," he said to himself. "Pretend this is something you see every day."

Ms. Bird of Paradise came to where he was and only smiled.

"Hey Ms. BOP--nice to see you this morning. How are you?"

Ms. BOP's sudden laugh could be heard throughout the building. "How am I?" She questioned before laughing again. "Oh, you can always make me laugh, Mr. Dev." And then she got down closer to where he was, and looking him in the eyes she said with kindness he needed right now, "I think the question is how are you?"

Taz couldn't fake it any longer. The casual-but-tough-guy persona he was so good at using, wasn't available this time. He struggled to say the words, and looked up to the ceiling to keep the tears from leaking out. "I think I'm having the worst day of my life, and it's not even 8:30 a.m."

With a smile Ms. BOP nodded, and then said, "I've noticed you a lot this year Taz. You seem to deal with more of your share of difficult relationships. I'm wondering if you're ready for some help."

With his 'white flag' in the shape of lined paper resting on the tile beside him, and knowing that the troubled feelings he'd been living with for far too long we're worse, not better, he bravely confessed, "I am."

"Well, that's what I wanted to hear," Ms. BOP said, right before her smile beamed as brightly as the sun.

Helping Taz back to his feet, she said out loud, **"This I-ITness has a cure!"**

"Excuse me, Ms. BOP--this what?"

"Don't you worry Mr. Dev. You'll understand soon enough." And with his bag on her shoulder, and motioning for him to follow, she smiled warmly and said with a wink, "I know a guy."

Transforming the Cardboard in Our Lives

Repeating what was said a few pages back, "*Seeing* is Being quintessential." Seeing correctly, truthfully, **is the magic pencil shavings that bring any cardboard cutout to life.**

Our lives may not *always* feel as nightmarish as Mr. Taz Dev's did just now, but to some degree or another, we live with cardboard in our lives, and the difficulty that arises with those cutouts is very real.

Any troubled relationship--anytime we are seeing another as a 5' x 3' x .25" corrugated obstacle in our world--brings negative emotions that permeate every other aspect of our lives.[6] There is no hiding from those unwanted feelings. Ignoring or suppressing or

---

[6] Bonds that Make Us Free, by C. Terry Warner

pretending them away doesn't work. Running from them isn't possible either. We've learned all too well that "there ain't no place that far."[7]

Troubled feelings that turn the people in our lives into I-IT mannequins, rob us of time and energy that could be more productively spent in 'Q-Living' ways. Troubled feelings rob us tremendously of efficiency and productivity in work and life. Our happiness suffers. In fact, the cardboard equation could be written thus: The amount of cardboard you interact with daily is directly proportional to the amount of unhappiness you feel. And it works in the inverse as well: No cardboard? Know awesome! (Know cardboard? No fun.)

It's worth restating then, that learning the art of being fully present with others (in order to see them correctly *and bring them to life*), IS the most important thing we can do to be the person we want to be! Everything else, as noble an endeavor as it may be, is secondary. It is the code that unlocks the door to *being* our *very best* selves, as often as we possibly can. It is the 'Q key' that brings <u>Humanity</u> and <u>Presence</u> together in our being, that we may live quintessentially, every single day!

. . . .

For more information about transforming your I-IT relationships into REAL, living, deeply meaningful, harmonious interactions, please find me--Mike Forsyth-- on all social media channels, as well as at my website: <u>mikeforsyth.com</u> or <u>liveintheq.com</u>. Training in various formats is available. Customizable opportunities are waiting!

---

[7] Disney's *Song of the South*

Ms. BOP is a reference! And now Taz Dev is too.

CHAPTER 6
A Quintessential Impact

How Many Apples?

I remember the first time I was ever asked the question, "How many apples can you get from one apple seed?" One teeny tiny little dark brown seed sitting so meekly in the middle of your hand.

Have you ever thought about that before? One hundred apples? Let's get crazy--five hundred apples! "No--wait..." *thinking out loud as you scratch your chin and look up with a furrowed brow...* "Maybe by... planting *every* seed from *every* apple that was produced from the *first* tree that grew from our *first* little seed..."

If your answer is a billion apples, you're WAY off. Try infinity apples! Infinity *plus* infinity apples!

You may call that exponential, or compounding growth. Scientifically and mathematically, however, that's often called 'insane exponential' or 'crazy compounding' growth! You go from one to one gabillion in only a few seasons.

And that's Quintessentialism. It is an ever-growing, expanding, enlarging cycle that radiates outward and builds upon itself.

This axiom of *loving in the now* is a potent, forceful and combustible engine for good. Its reach is limitless. Powerful relationships built on positive connectivity grow outward and upward. The smallest Q moment can lead to an infinite number of others. These tertiary moments start their own chain reactions until entire office floors, then departments, then complete organizations, businesses and companies, homes and neighborhoods and on and on are fundamentally transformed--one life, one relationship, one quintessential moment at a time!

"Cue the 'Q Story'!"

It was the spring of my sophomore year of high school a LONG time ago, in a city far, far away. (Okay, Orem, Utah--Orem High School--1990! *Go Tigers!*)

I came from a junior high in which most of my closest friends at the time were all heading off to the rival high school across the way. Total bummer that our junior high fed two different schools, and easily seventy-five percent went the other direction. I was--in a big way--starting over with my social circle. I had the challenge of meeting new friends, starting over, and trying to figure it all out like SO many of us do at that difficult time of life. I wasn't doing particularly well at it either, you should know. High school was three years for us, so by the springtime of my first year, as a sophomore, I was still pretty dang expendable. Skinny, shy and in-se-CURE! Looking back now, it might've been THE most insecure season of my entire life.

It was at that time that I got a call from my amazing uncle who lived in our same town. Uncle Dave invited me to go with their family to Lake Powell in Southern Utah for Spring Break weekend. They had a houseboat, and I was welcome to join them.

I remember being on the phone in the kitchen, thinking it over carefully. *His kids were younger*--the closest to me in age (that I'd be hanging out with) was Josh: a 6th grader. "Let's see," I thought, "the deepest blue skies against the reddest cliffs against the most dazzling blue water ever, combined with.... hanging out with my kid cousin that was four years younger. Hmmm."

"I think I'll go, Uncle Dave. Thanks for the invitation." I figured I could have a good time. Kick around in the boat, relax, take in the sun, and play with the little cousin. I'd be the oldest and help out, and life would be pretty good for a few days.

And that's how it seemed, until... we were half way there! Three hours into a six-hour drive, I'm talking with my cousins in the back of the motorhome we were riding in. I learned from my cousin Kara that it wasn't going to be just their family and me. Uncle Dave and Aunt Kathleen had failed to tell me they had also invited two other families to join them! What was worse--what was horrible news--was that there were going to be two 19-year-old Orem High graduates coming down!

Now, I can imagine that this is very difficult for most of you reading to understand, why exactly this was such tragic news for me. But it was! I was in NO mood to be in the proximity of older, stronger, taller, cooler strangers. I was going away for the weekend to *escape* my insecurity problems, not to be thrown headfirst into them! Had I been given full disclosure about this trip on the phone, I know exactly what I would've said! I would have graciously declined, hung up the phone and went back to being left alone, hiding in my insecure bubble.

And now it was too late! No turning back! There was nothing I could do. I was stuck. And I knew right then and there that this was going to be one *terrible, horrible, no good, very bad* weekend. (Self-conscious, huh? I hadn't even met these guys yet, but I was already in the Me-Zone toward them. I-IT to the max! Self-absorbed.)

I could picture them too: all decked out in the latest boating attire, trendy, like all the cool seniors looked to me. But only cooler! These two were even a year older than all of them! They had each other too. Best friends. They'd be the bosses, and I'd be unnoticed and left to play with 6th-grader-Josh while they had all the fun. Good grief!

I remember when I first saw them. Uh, they were even *cooler* than I had IMAGINED! We were loading the houseboat with gear from our vehicles, walking back and forth over a narrow plank from the boat to the dock. That's when they passed me coming, while I was planning on crossing the plank. I waited for them to come across before I started up. Gargoyle shades, lifeguard tank tops, tan, chiseled--need I say more? Oh!...can't forget the high school hair flopping on their heads, the kind that every dude eventually loses! My initial assessment of the situation had been spot on. File this weekend away under the word "awful" and roll the cabinet drawer closed!

Later, I was on the top of the houseboat eating my dinner. (Think of a floating shoe box with a blue carpet top, and a white metal railing all around, close to 40 feet long, maybe 15 feet wide.) I was on the flat blue roof, next to the guard rail, sitting by myself on a chair in one corner. My sleeping bag and pillow were rolled out beside me, next to my cousin's. I was eating Kentucky Fried Chicken, (as we called it back then) coleslaw, and mashed potatoes and gravy on a paper plate, and yes--I had my spork. I was wallowing in a deep bath of self-pity and counting the minutes until all of this would be over. On the far side of the houseboat, kiddie-corner from me, were the two older guys, laying out their sleeping bags and talking. I kept my head down and pretended not to notice them.

Before I realized what had happened, one of these dudes had walked directly over to where I was sitting, and while standing over me reached out his hand.

"Hey man, how are you? What's your name?"

I couldn't believe this was happening. I practically froze. I looked up and said, "Uh... hey. My name is Mike."

"Your name is Mike!? No way! You won't believe this, man, but *my* name is Mike too! And that dude over there--*his* name is Mike! Hey Mike," he yelled to his buddy, "get over here and meet Mike."

"And immediately, here comes the other Mike. (And then there were two!)

"Hey Mike, nice to meet you!" said Mike.

Now both Mikes are standing over me, asking me who I was, how I knew Dave and Kathleen and taking some time to learn more about a scrawny, shy sophomore kid they did not know.

After a couple minutes, Mike One asked, "So is this your pillow and sleeping bag?" pointing to the items beside me.

And before I could answer, Mike One did something that stopped time for me. I watched as he reached down and picked up my bag and pillow, and while carrying it away with him, said, "So let's go ahead and take this over here where we are. You can sleep beside us. We'll grab your cousin's too. We've brought some games to play, and you can be on my team. Mike's sister--who's pretty cute-- is also with us and you'll have to meet her. We'll have a lot of fun."

Fast forward three hours. Fast forward past the games we played that night, the fun, the laughing, the talking. Stop the tape about where you see me, laying inside my bag with it pulled up tight under my chin. Everyone else looks to be asleep. But I'm still awake, gazing at the stars.

And zoom in closer now, as I'm looking heavenward, thinking some very powerful thoughts to myself. They sounded a little like this:

"I think I have just met the two coolest 19-year-olds there ever, ever were. I have met the two coolest guys on this planet."

And the second thought was this:

"I want to be just like them."

. . . .

Today I'm retelling this story almost 30 years from the time it happened. And for as long as it's been, that memory doesn't seem to fade for me. That quintessential moment, when Mike and Mike were fully present with me--when I was the one within their reach-- when I was the one they saw as a 'thou,' ... it changed my life. The impact is immeasurable.

I have had a career in education. Along with classes and assemblies, I have taught thousands of kids. I've presented at summer camps, youth conferences and other learning seminars. I've spoken in many different settings, in front of many different people, and I've told this story many times. Even when I haven't shared the story, many of my themes, topics, and strongly-held beliefs have been shaped and validated by that potent experience: when Mike and Mike were their very best selves.

And now it's in my first book. My first book about the limitless, infinite power that can explode from being in the moment, with the one you're with! And the impact, and the ripples and the seeds, and the apples and the orchards that start in the smallest of moments.

"Is this your bag? Is this your pillow, right here?"

Beyond telling the story many times, I've been hyper-aware throughout my life to do my best--despite many fallbacks--to look for the one who's eating alone.

The next morning was just the same. There was never a time that entire weekend when it was 'them' and 'the rest', it was always 'us'. Everyone who was there would agree.

I found them both on social media ten years ago when a bolt of lightning zapped my thoughts with, "Hey! I bet Mike and Mike are out there on Facebook somewhere!"

I reached out minutes later and learned that one of them lived... twenty *houses* away! No joke!

We made arrangements for him and his family to come to my place, to meet my wife and kids. I made sure to take the time I needed beforehand to retell my family the story, and to let them know just how special the individual coming over to our home was to me, and how he had changed my life forever.

"Sometimes when I consider the tremendous consequences from little things, a touch on the shoulder, a smile, or a wink of an eye, I am tempted to think, there are no little things." -Bruce Barton

"No act of kindness, no matter how small, is ever wasted." -Aesop

From left to right: Mike Forsyth, Mike Coles & Mike Rieske
Lake Powell, April 1990

CHAPTER 7
The Q and You--Seeing Yourself Quintessentially

A Me-Zone Movie Makeover

"And...*Cut!*" shouts the director on the set of *Ocean's 14*, somewhere on the Fort Knox Army base in Kentucky. "Let's break for lunch! We begin shooting the ventriloquist scene in one hour! George and Brad, don't be late for make-up. We need you back here in sixty minutes sharp!"

Brad Pitt and George Clooney are unstrapped from where they've been hanging, dressed in Armani suits and Gucci shades, filming a critical scene in what will ultimately be the greatest heist in U.S. history. The government's largest vault has been broken into!

George and Brad have a seat at a small round table in a secluded corner of the set, ready to chow down on some dripping steak sandwiches before they're off to the next mind-blowing con! If you only knew!

"I am loving this movie, Brad!" says George with his mouth full. "I thought we would never hit one out of the park like *Ocean's 11* again, but I think this is it!"

"Completely agree," Brad mutters. "We've done it! And the surprise ending--Oh my GOSH!"

Clooney jumps in. "Everybody's thinking we'll go right--and then we go LEFT! Totally amazing, bro!"

"We go so left, it's right!" laughs Brad.

"OH, SO RIGHT!" They burst out saying to each other with a high-five!

"Oh man. That was funny," moments later, says George. "Right!?"

"RIGHT!" laughs Brad.

More chuckles and eye drying.

"But seriously, Brad, can I be honest with you for a minute?" George Clooney finally gets himself together and looks around to make sure they're alone.

"Yeah, man. What's up?" Brad responds.

"It's the craziest thing, but I've never felt better in my life about who I am these days, and it's all because of a cool little book I just read. Wondered if you'd heard of it. It's called *Live in the Q* by Mike Forsyth."

"No! But dang, Cloon--congrats on actually reading a book! Did you take a picture?" asks Brad as he licks some sauce off his fingers, still smiling about the banter.

"You're hilarious, bro. Okay, I'll be honest--Julia Roberts read it to me first, but *anyway*...I'm so glad she did! This Mike guy, in his book, says that when we're living in the moment, really trying to be present, AND caring for those around us, that's when we're our *very best selves*. Suddenly I'm Mr. Nice Guy everywhere I go. I've never felt better!"

"So *that's* it! I thought it was my 'joke-a-day,'" said Brad, pointing with his sandwich to his phone, before another bite.

"Hey man. This changed me! You're lucky I'm sharing. So, here's the best part: he explains that it's also just as important to see yourself accurately too! If you're not seeing yourself as you 'really are,' truthfully, then you can be too hard on yourself, hang on to mistakes far too long, and not allow yourself to be present with others, because you're not actually present with yourself. He says when we're not liking ourselves at any particular time, then how can we look outward toward others?"

"Cloon--what? You've had problems liking yourself?" Brad says, taking a sip of his beverage.

George takes a deep cleansing breath and then says, looking down at his now patiently waiting sandwich, "*Ocean's 12*, man. I just haven't been able to get my head right since then. Dude, that was a terrible movie! I mean, I *knew* the script still needed major work, and I signed off on production anyway! And then, all my second-guessing bled into my acting! Oh, you could see the worry as clear as the salt and pepper scruff on my face. And my smolder didn't have it like it did before, and..."

"Are you serious!? You've been beating yourself up since *Ocean's 12*!?"

"We let the whole world down Brad! I mean, everybody LOVED *Ocean's 11*! And I get it--it was soooo good! Seriously, it was like my high-water mark. And then..."

Taking the last bite of his sandwich, Brad says, "Gosh, that's news, man. I would've thought *Batman Forever* would've pushed you off the cliff, but no..."

"That was nothing compared to this Pitt," says George, now playing with his food. "*Ocean's 12* has haunted me ever since. And then I was praying I could come correct with *Ocean's 13*, but… ay ya yai!"

"Anyway--this book has given me a whole new life! I think you really need to--"

"Cloon--I have something to tell you, pal," Brad interrupts, and then looks away for a minute, slowly wiggling his fingers free of bread crumbs and then pulling his eyes tight to stop the tears… "Me too."

"What!?" George chokes on his sandwich, eyes wide open. "You bash yourself over *12* too!?"

"You should read my journal, Cloon," confesses Pitt. "I swear every page has something about it. I mean, how do you forgive yourself for something like that!? My whole inner world fell apart, and I'm still trying to clear my head of those cobwebs. I've never told a soul George, cuz I figured no one would understand. I figured everyone else was stronger than me, that they were the ones with the mental toughness. They could handle it. Turns out, maybe we'd all be surprised at just who struggles Georgie."

As busy as the giant movie set is, full of people, running, working, lifting and carrying movie set things, nobody notices the two friends tucked quietly away in the corner, sitting at a round table, wearing Armani suits and looking oh, so cool, but so tender and vulnerable and real underneath it all.

"George," says Brad, breaking the quiet, looking up slowly. "That book… *Live in the Q*, is it?"

"Ya," George mutters.

"Will you read it to me?"

George nods his head ever so subtly, as if in wistful thought. And then here comes that George Clooney smile and twinkle when he says, "You got it brother! We'll start this afternoon!

At that moment, a blaring voice over the intercom can be heard. "Mr. Clooney and Mr. Pitt, you're wanted in make-up. Mr. Clooney and Mr. Pitt--please find your way to make-up."

Low Q High

My 20th year high school reunion was a blast! Not that I wasn't nervous and fretting beforehand--don't get me wrong. But once we got there and settled in, it sure was fun to see so many people from so long ago.

The biggest surprise of all? After the abundant hair loss noticeable everywhere--is how shocked I was to learn through a few conversations with several people just how *insecure* everybody was back in high school!

I couldn't believe it. I remember chatting with one guy in particular. To me, back in the day--he had it ALL: the cute girl, the incredibly fun personality, and tons of friends. I thought--if anybody was secure in who they were back in high school, it had to be him. To hear him, twenty years later, talk about what was really going on between his ears was eye opening. Others said the same thing. I remember thinking then that someday this would go in a book of mine!

Amazing, huh? Back in the day we had all walked the halls, acting and pretending like we had it figured out. And unbeknownst to any of us, we were all struggling in our own private universe inside, to one degree or another. And I'm sure we've all wondered since, has any of that really changed?

. . . .

We can't be in the We-Zone when we're grumpy or ornery, mad or upset. Those feelings are 'good-as-gold' indicators that we're I-ITing it all over the place. And oftentimes, our being upset and cranky comes not from what others do to us, but rather from what we do to ourselves, and from the self-talk we heap upon the already-too-big pile of self-accusing lies we're collecting every day about who we think we are.

Not only can we find ourselves stuck in troubled relationships with others, we can also, and even more easily, it seems, find ourselves stuck in a troubled relationship with... _ourselves!_ In this chapter we tackle the challenge of getting unstuck from the relationship we have with possibly our hardest critic. We'll work on seeing ourselves as the THOU that others often do, and the way Martin Buber would suggest; and NOT as people "subject[ed] to coordination...describable, analyzable, classifiable... an aggregate of qualities... [a] system of coordinates."

I'm no psychologist, (although I do have a doctorate in Quintessentialism!) but my crazy life-long quest to understand relationships has led me to a distillation of three keys that can help us better understand ourselves, and to be kinder to ourselves. **See the YOU inside of you**. And thus, live in the Q more often.

Separate from Our *Thoughts*

As Eckhart Tolle alluded to and helped those listening to him realize, we can *separate* (verb) from our thoughts because we are *separate* (adjective) from our thoughts. In other words, we are NOT the thoughts that come and go in and out of our minds--like clouds come and go in the sky. Jack Kornfield, a favorite mindfulness teacher today, describes our thoughts as a--(Can you guess? You've heard it before. Good job!)--as a leaf floating on top of and swirling along with a meandering, bubbling and bouncing stream.

Like the leaf in the stream of our mind, we can identify a thought when we first notice it floating its way into our consciousness. We do so by acknowledging it, without blame or accusation, judgement or fear. We simply point it out to ourselves, saying something like, "Oh, well here's an interesting thought. How peculiar to have it come through at this time of day." Or, maybe, "Whattup bro!? Long time no see!"

We have the ability to see it from various angles, to stand apart from it. To ask questions--if we choose--about it, and to even let it gently float on by. How long we entertain or become fixed on the thought in any way, is up to us! [Got a problem with that? Talk to my buddy Victor Frankl! He wrote the book on this--literally, after he survived several concentration camps during World War Two. He discovered in a moment of epiphany, while in torturous conditions that man always has freedom: freedom to choose one's thoughts. It's titled *Man's Search for Meaning*. It's a must read! (And my editor emphatically agrees!)]

"Don't believe everything you think. Thoughts are just that--thoughts." - Allan Lokos

"If you really want to remove a cloud from your life, you do not make a big production of it, you just relax and remove it from your thinking. That's all there is to it." -Richard Bach

We are the only known species of living things on Earth that can do this. For as intelligent as we have discovered that so many of our animal friends are, not one has ever been on record for having asked a question about their own thinking! (Asking for a potato chip while under the table, maybe. But I digress. "Just one more potato chip? Please? Just one more? Please? Thanks. Just *one* more potato chip?")

At the lowest point in his life, as he describes it, Eckhart Tolle was able to stand apart from his thinking and look at a specific thought objectively. It was the turning point in his life, and the genesis of his career as a teacher of mindfulness practices. The thought was this: "I cannot live with myself." His question? "Who is the 'I' and who is 'myself?' One of these must not be real, must not be me."

It takes practice, and yes, it helps when things are quiet and still, but even so--we can at every moment--see a thought, hear a thought, become acquainted with a thought, and find peace in knowing that that little, or big, or scary, or hurtful, or insecure, or mean, or nagging, or repetitious, or habitual thing floating by is NOT who we are! We are *separate* (adjective) from them, and being mindful of that, we can *separate* (verb) from them as well.

Separate from our Feelings

Like thoughts--our feelings and emotions are either intruders or invited guests! They are NOT you, nor can they ever be you. When we say that we are mad, or we are upset, or we are happy;

yes, people understand what we mean. But in a very real sense, you exist before a feeling, after a feeling and even outside of a feeling.

You are not the flu, are you? If you are not the common cold, then you are not the frustrated, not the embarrassed, and not the furious. Many of these feelings arise for reasons we discuss in *See-to-Be* and we can learn to do with them exactly as we do with our thoughts: identify them, acknowledge them, be curious about them, and separate ourselves from them cognitively. We can also learn to let many of them go, let them float further downstream until they're gone.

Remember, feelings are graphable. You are not. Feelings are describable, countable, sortable, listable, chart-able, and plottable. You are beyond anything of the sort. The I-YOU you is infinite in every direction. Try listing that on a chalkboard or writing all that in a notebook!

My lovely and amazing wife will read this for the first time and laugh. She'll say, "*You* wrote this book? Hmm. This guy doesn't sound anything like you, babe."

"I know. I know, Tweetie." (Me, with a smirk and rolling my eyes from across the room.)

Hey! I told you already, I didn't choose Quintessentialism! This book and Quintessentialism chose me! I'm just the imperfect means by which it made its introduction to the world. And believe me, I am trying so very hard to improve in every area that I write about here--every day!

Exhibit A: I was birthed and raised by the most loving, self-sacrificing woman in all the world! Hey, mom! How are you? Whaddaya think of this book so far, huh? I know, right!?

She'll be the first to tell you that she kept one clean closet! And bedroom! And kitchen! And 'nother closet! She made our beds so dang perfectly. She hung up our clothes so dang perfectly, too. Hangers were evenly spaced! And the wash rag on the bathroom counter was--yup--perfectly folded and always at 90 degrees to edges of sinks and counters. Right angles were all 'right around you' at the Forsyths! (So right it was wrong!)

True story--(sorry, Mom) the boyfriends and in-laws visiting would like to play with her a bit. Right before she'd walk in the front door, they'd mess up the ruffle on the edge of a floor rug, and then turn a picture sitting on a bookshelf just a bit. You know--mix up the 90's and 45's. Something at a 78-degree angle for crying out loud!

She'd walk in and say in a cheery voice, "Well hi, everyone!" (Bends down and straightens ruffle.) "So how is everyone today? What have you all been up to?" (Straightens picture on bookshelf.) "What? What's so funny?"

Well guess what? I didn't realize until *after* I was married that my sweet mother was a one-of-a-kind, unplottable, uncategorical, unduplicable, unchartable superwoman! Everyone else is what you'd call, "normal."

Yup, I married the most amazing normal woman you've ever met! Our closets are normal, behind the couch is normal, our bedroom floor is normal, the kitchen sink is normal, my unfolded socks are normal--and our disagreements are normal. (*Wait for it...story coming.*)

One day I was finishing up the vacuuming: dancing around while singing along to an R.E.M. tune in my head, enjoying life. And then like any normal person would, I went to my normal junk closet to put our normal vacuum away, to have normal junk fall out and land on my normal head.

That's called a trigger. (*I paid a lot of money to learn that word.*)

And those pesky triggers have a cunning way of turning happy moments of dancing with the vacuum into instant and unwanted irritations! ...Aaargh!

This next metaphor is 100 percent mine. And our marriage counselor was impressed.

"Ya know, Sigmond, it finally came to me! I figured it out. It's like a bomb. It's like someone just walked up out of nowhere and handed me a big black bowling-ball-sized bomb (*just like you'd see in the cartoons, complete with a happy little fuse that's lit like a sparkler*). I didn't ask for it--I didn't *want* it--I didn't go looking for it... Sheesh! I was in a good mood just moments before, and PRESTO--feelings of absolute annoyance. Plopped right in my hands. Now what?"

"Ooo, this is great Mike, I'm taking notes, keep going," says Sigmond.

"So yeah... I've learned I can't *hide* the bomb, oh no! I can't shove it down my sweater or put it under my jacket. Believe me, I've tried that puh-lenty of times before. It goes something like this...

"'Are you okay, babe?' I imitate my wife's angelic voice, speaking to me. 'You seem quiet.'"

"Me? Just peachy, Tweetie. (*Responding with a Han Solo twist.*) 'Everything's perfectly alright now. We're fine, we're all fine here, now, thank you. How are you?'[8]"

Sigmond cracks up, bouncing his feet! "Oh, this is awesome! 'Luke, we're gonna have company!' HA! So, then what does your wife say?" He's leaning forward.

"She says sweetly, 'Oh, okay. Well, I'm only asking because we haven't talked in about, well, about a week now and uh… is that smoke coming out of your left ear?'"

Sigmond bursts out his best guffaw. "Fabulous! This is a terrific story! Yes, no WAY was that working bro--keeping quiet. 'Buried feelings never die.' Good book![9] So then what?" he asks, trying to get serious again.

"KABOOM! That's what! KA--*BIBBITY- BOBBITY*--BOOM!"

"GUH--!" (*Waiting for Sigmond to catch his breath. His sudden guffaw hadn't 'fawed'.*)

"Laugh it up, fuzz ball!"[10]

(*Now waiting* longer *for Sigmond to catch his breath.*)

"Sigmond, breathe. Inhale! No doctors die on my watch!"

He motions for me to keep talking.

"Ya, so major explosion every time. Just wait long enough and … Mt. Vesuvius!

---

[8] *Star Wars: A New Hope*
[9] <u>Feelings Buried Alive Never Die</u>, by Karol K. Truman
[10] *Star Wars: Empire Strikes Back*

"So, what do I learn? I learn real fast that I can't hide or ignore these feelings and simply pray and hope and wish they go away. (Heaven knows I have tried!) They NEVER do, Doc! They just keep fermenting.

"But Doc! I CAN'T TALK ABOUT IT EITHER! I learned just as fast that it doesn't work to go up to my wife and say, 'See this bomb here? It's kinda *your* fault.' "

"Doc?" Mike questions Sigmond, as he's watching him try to pick himself up off the floor, "Dude, pull yourself together, man."

"And it doesn't matter how sweetly I say it, either. 'Babe, cutie, sweetheart--you're so awesome. See this crazy trigger bomb here that I'm holding. I really don't want it to explode all over us so I'll try super hard to say this as kindly as I can. I know we've got three kids and you just had a baby, but will you please, pretty please, clean that junk closet? Thank you. Love you. G-night.'

"Can't you see, I need help here, Doc!?" I yell, as he runs for the bathroom because his tissue box is empty. "No matter which stove I touch, I'm burned! The bomb explodes if I *do*. It explodes if I *don't*. I'm trapped! AND I DIDN'T ASK FOR IT, DOC! I was in an awesome mood just seconds before! Life sabotaged *me*, Doc! But maybe today isn't the day for answers, huh, Doc?" I shout at the half-closed door.

Moments later Sigmond returned to his chair. His face and nose are red, his eyes dryer but still teary. His hands are filled with paper towels.

. . . .

As soon as his hiccups are under control, Sigmond begins to teach me that there is a way to talk about your *feelings*, with your wife, by isolating those feelings, standing apart from them, acknowledging them, and getting through the rough moment as the feeling comes and goes, all while you're holding hands[11], waiting it out, and letting it pass--with each other.

It isn't you. It isn't him or her. You are *separate* from your feelings. They often come unexpectedly. And like our leaf-like thoughts floating down a stream, you can s*eparate* from them too--together.

(*Sound of sparkling fuse being extinguished.*) "Tsssssss."

(*Sound of Mike finding peace in his life after many years.*) "Ahhhhhh!"

(*Sound of my wife reading this for the first time.*) "Whaaaat!?"

Separate from Our Labels

[See to Be *is a live training I've created that explores how we can better see each other truthfully, remove the I-IT cardboard in our relationships and thus live life more often in the Q. What follows is an original activity that I include in this training, as part of the 'See thy Self' section of the workshop. I am happy to share it here: knowing that it can make a difference in the ability of each of us to see ourselves the way we need to and to find the Q in these otherwise difficult moments, when our reaction-prone behavior is put to the test. May it bless us here, now and forever, regardless of whether our paths cross again in the future. Here's to our best selves, my friends!*]

If you'll indulge me for one second, I'd like to point out that my understanding of what comes next was revealed during a time of struggle: when a particular place in a book I was reading became very difficult to figure out. I'll forever remember where I was when

---

[11] <u>Hold Me Tight</u>, by Dr. Sue Johnson

a lightbulb turned on: after many times flipping back and forth between the pages, I could instantly see how to better understand this concept and how I could teach it to others.

I'm hoping you've all had the glorious experience of writing your name on one of those "HELLO, my name is _____" sticky name-tags, so you can become better acquainted with your 3rd cousin, twice removed. Or maybe it happens at that Backyard Chicken Coop group you attend regularly.

Well today--like those good times--we're busting out the labels! Grab your marker, and on the front--instead of your name--*this* is what you need to write:

"Being (a) _____ affirms (or validates) my worth."

Now, assign it a value of 1-100 and write that number in some corner of the sticker.

Okay, for those scratching your head, saying "Uh...my what is firm?" let me explain further. Each of us--if given time to really mull it over--can think of qualities, traits, interests, and talents that are important to us, and that we identify with in meaningful ways. Often people know us and even recognize us for many of these attributes. Our reputation among co-workers, colleagues, friends, family, and the community can often lean heavily on these qualities. Here are a few examples to get you started:

- Being an accomplished tamborine player affirms my worth.
- Being a quota-hitting sales representative affirms my worth.
- Being eye-catching in a bathing suit affirms my worth.
- Being right affirms my worth.

- Being an accomplished athlete (or musician or cook) affirms my worth.
- Being wealthy affirms my worth.
- Being un-disappointing affirms my worth.
- Being better than others (another) affirms my worth.
- Being the best affirms my worth.
- Being honest and a person of integrity affirms my worth.
- Being someone with lots of 'likes' and 'retweets' affirms my worth.

Okay, now it's your turn! Let's create a few labels--don't stop at just one. Make a handful! Lay them out in front of you. Choose some that rank very high on the 1-100 scale, and also choose some that rank low.

Can you think of an attribute that might even rank at a zero for you? I can think of one for me. "Being an excellent guitar player affirms my worth." (I don't play the guitar at all!) What about one that ranks high? For me I'd say, "Being likable or accepted affirms my worth." I wish it wasn't so, but I'd have to give that one close to 85, 90 or more points.

Got 'em? And you're looking at them all proudly? Excellent!

Now... before you put them on...Turn them over! Surprise! This label is unlike any label you've ever seen before, huh? What do you notice? That's right--*another label* on the back! It's a two-in-one! But look closely, this side has a different phrase written on it. It says:

"But NOT being a(n) _____, subtracts _____ value points from my worth."

Before anything else, write on this side in the second blank the same value between 1-100 that is written on the reverse side!

Next, fill in the first blank, using the characteristic or trait from the front. Here are a couple examples:

- But NOT being likable or accepted, subtracts 83 value points from my worth.
- But NOT being young and attractive, subtracts 45 value points from my worth.

Have you filled out both sides? Now pretend to stick them on! Go ahead--it's you! You own them, they are yours. Wear them proudly. It's who--in many respects--you believe you are!

Alright, what I say next is called psychology. It'll pass soon! We won't let it scare us! Hopefully it's been made simpler to understand, to thus be better applied in a more helpful way, to the challenges we often have of fearfully seeing ourselves inaccurately.

Somehow or another, some way or another we've formulated opinions (or labels) about ourselves, and attached our worth to them. It might've happened early in life, before we can even remember. These labels may be the result of our upbringing or born from achievements or recognition: things we have long clung to. Maybe they were forged in the furnace of extreme emotional affliction. However, it's happened, these are labels we wear.

And the ones we've assigned high values to, these labels we defend!

For they can be challenged!

Life puts them up for debate, sometimes from out of the blue. And despite our best efforts to the contrary, society or even those closest to us seem to form different opinions about who we are, and the labels we wear. Yes, the world wants to be the judge over you and me, two people they know so very little about.

Now… for low-value labels, whoop-de-do! Easy come, easy go. "You didn't like my guitar playing? HA! Neither did I!" Or, "I'm not really good at card games? That's hilarious! What was your first clue? That I couldn't tell which side is up?"

But for the other labels--the labels with the big numbers written on each side--the slightest perceived judgment can really sting! It can hurt us oh so terribly. It hurts because… there's more for us at stake than just a sticky label. It's our self-perceived *worth* that's on the line! A huge pile of our value--equal to its weight in gold and rubies--has been threatened. That's a lot to lose!

It hurts for another reason too. In some cases, when the high number correlates with a perceived talent or accomplishment or self-proclaimed identity, it means we're being questioned or challenged, or accused of having failed at our *strength!* We're seemingly losing on our turf, while doing what we're *best* at! It can mean we've potentially failed at doing what we're known for, or what we feel is most important! And that would be a major fail! And a long way to fall.

I heard it said once that in the final analysis, we allow our lives to be governed by only two emotions--love and fear.[12] Losing 'big numbers' my friends, (or maybe even not so big) which we perceive as our worth--IS FEAR! The seeming potential of losing our life-sustaining, reputation-making, confidence-giving and importance-validating labels are at the *least,* worth fighting for, and at the *most,* downright horrific.

---

[12] Elisabeth Kubler-Ross & David Kessler from "Life Lessons: Two Experts on Death and Dying Teach Us About the Mysteries of Life and Living"

So, boy, do we fight! Like a mother bear we fight. With reflexes like a jungle cat. We have to! The mere *thought* of losing in the battle over a priceless label is unbearable enough. It's our *identity*, it's who we *are*, and maybe to some... a label can even be more cherished than life itself. We'll fight to the end to save it, to protect it, to secure it to ourselves once again.

"How dare you think I'm not cut out for this crossing guard position!"

"Not good work? Really? How can you say that!? Show me once where I colored outside the lines!?"

"Can you believe that's what she said!? I know! How absolutely ignorant! Like she knows anything about plastic surgery."

"I didn't make a mistake! If there are three apples, and then someone takes two apples, then he has two apples! There're two apples remaining that he has! Good grief--the ignorance of some people!"

. . . .

The quickest way that I know of, to jump head first into the Me-Zone, and by-golly stay there (!) is by defending and fighting for our labels. We instantly react, throw up our guard, scramble for our shield, grab the sword, and swing away.

Here's where I need you to read slowly again.

Those labels that we are so afraid of losing, are NOT you and me.

In the same way that you are more than your thoughts, you are more than your feelings. And you are also more than the labels you wear.

You exist outside of these labels, as hard as it can be to believe, at times. You *can* stand apart from these labels. You *can* see them as a separate entity with a life of their own.

Yes, we have responsibilities, we have roles to play that demand our attention and concern. We have bills to pay and children to raise. I know something about the crippling pressures of providing for a family. I know about tough crowds, losing the sale, falling short at the end of Q2, Q3 and Q4. I know a thing about the end of ropes. "Provider" and "Father" are two of the most significant and unrelenting labels I wear.

But we can stand separate from those labels--and every other label-- to a very real degree. We *can* detach our 'innate Martin Buber'--our *intrinsic*, unlimited, unplottable worth--from the *extrinsic* job we're doing; the vocational circumstance we're navigating; or the 'No, I am NOT doing that!' familial situation we're surviving.

By doing so, we are being present. By doing so, we are practicing healthy mindfulness techniques. We are ALSO (!) at the same time showing concern for and giving care to the person that is struggling in the moment, within our reach--ourselves! We are *living in the Q!*

One more story. Eeek--I can't help myself!

I was in a hotel room one morning--far from home--in Omak, Washington. I was getting ready to take a long drive from there to Spokane. At the time, I was a traveling salesman and I'd seen better days. Okay, I'd seen better years. The pressure at the time was intense. That morning an email was delivered to my inbox. It was bad news. I had lost a big sale. Another email came in. More of the same bad news, but with a different client. They come in threes, don't they? A third heartbreaking email (or text) or something--I cannot remember exactly--popped up with words that meant more or less, goodbye. Those three at once--at that tough time in my life--were enough to... uh... put me down for the count.

Do you need more details? The comforter on my bed was a pinkish floral pattern, and my face was in it. At that moment, it seemed as if I--not my world--but I, Mike Forsyth, might unravel. That's the best word I could *ever* find to describe it. I felt like there was nothing holding me together, and if I moved wrong, or got up too fast, I would come all undone.

What to do.

(long pause)

"I am more than this label, I am more than this label.
"I am NOT this label I wear.
"I stand apart from this label.
"My worth does not exist inside this label."

Remember this next one? *(I share for emphasis, trying only to better convey how I was feeling, and what I was expressing.)*

"[I am NOT] subject to coordination...describable, analyzable, classifiable... an aggregate of qualities... [Mike] knows no system of coordinates."

I think God was telling me the same.

Standing apart from these labels, we more accurately see them for what they are, and we see ourselves for who WE are.

With this new perspective, we *can* now "stand in relation" to ourselves, our labels and our fears. While in this quintessential state of being, we *can* now and simply, calmly and more beautifully honor the process of courageously moving forward, one small step at a time, and of bravely doing the next right thing. We *can* try our best to be our best, the best that we can. We can more fully live in the present, reach out to the one, even if it's us--*especially* if it's us... one isolated, and all-important moment at a time.

And we let go of the rest.

Including our labels.

We *separate* from our labels, because we're *separate* from our labels.

And...

Being <u>separate from my labels</u> affirms my worth.

CHAPTER 8
How to Begin – Q-ism Before Lunch!

Q-Mart

"So excited for the weekend, little brother! Wives taking off, just us with our kids. This has been a long time coming!" says Mike to his brother, Bill, while grabbing a shopping cart and heading into the grocery store.

"I can't agree more!" Bill replies. "We've waited for this forever, and now here it is! We'll grab these few items the girls asked us to pick up, get back to your place, kiss them goodbye... and get the dance-off started!!" *(Fist bumps.)*

"By the way," says Bill, as they stroll down the bread aisle, my friend John wanted me to ask you--'cuz he knew we'd be hanging out this weekend--what you'd suggest as being the one or two most important things a person could do to start *'Living in the Q'* right away. He wants to know how to begin--the right way, ya know? Get some good momentum quickly."

"Totally get it," responds Mike. "Great question. By the way--do your kids even eat bread? We've got wheat bread written down here. I'm trying to figure out why exactly."

"Not really, man," says Bill. "But whaddaya think about these? Mix it up this weekend?" *(Bill tosses him a box of cosmic fudge brownies with glow-in-the-dark sprinkles.)*

"Let's see," as Mike looks at the ingredients. "Enriched flour is the first thing listed. Flour's bread, that's for sure. Excellent thought, bro," says Mike, as he throws it into the cart. "On to the next!"

Start Where You're At

"So, regarding your friend, John's, question--tell him this, and by the way, I've written all this down in my book. I'll give you a copy to take back, so no need to remember everything right now. Tell him that you simply need to start right where you're at. Tell him that how you start *'living in the Q'* for the first time, is how you start *'living in the Q'* every time. And this is what I mean:

"Forget about yesterday, forget about an hour ago, forget about one minute ago even! When it comes to *'living in the Q'*, the past isn't counted. We move *forward!* There is no place like the present, and no better time than now. You start fresh, you start new--every time! It's the most forgiving thing you could ever engage in. And it's the most hope-filled activity you could ever attempt. You get an endless number of chances, an endless number of resets, and an endless number of do-overs. Tell him to imagine he has a little clicker counter in his hand--you know--the thing that you can push with your thumb and it keeps track of people walking by or something--have him imagine resetting that thing back to zeros immediately. And anytime he ever feels like resetting again--do it!"

"I like it brother. Now--granola, where the heck is the granola?"

"Can I say one more thing, Bill?"

"All day long, bro!"

"Tell him that all it takes to begin is to simply have the thought! Beginning to 'live in the Q' requires absolutely NO preparation, other than having the thought. That's it. If you can think it, you can do it. It is purely an *awareness* that you allow into your consciousness. Once it's there--you are ready!

"And about that awareness thing, let me explain. You know how when your regional boss is unexpectedly in the office for the day, everybody is very much *aware* of it? Magically the entire floor is... working (!) for once, at the same time! It's quiet and your supervisor is suddenly talking nicely to you?"

"That's hilarious."

"It's most definitely a part of your overall consciousness, even though you're thinking a million other things throughout the day.

"Or how about this," Mike continues. "You're feeling particularly put together, new shirt, the hair's right, the cologne's right and people can tell you've got a spring in your step?"

"Every day!"

"That's what it is! It's an awareness. It's a consciousness that puts you in the driver's seat. When you've got it, you're in it!"

"Bro! It's 'Q-consciousness!'" Bill says as he raises his hand for a five. (*Clap!*)

"I can't find this dang granola," says Bill.

"My kids think it's like eating rocks," offers Mike.

"Sawdust!"

"Seriously, man. Hey! Check this out!" Mike grunts as he throws Bill a 10-pound bag of Triple Chocolate Brownie Crunch with Marshmallows. "Now that's called, 'Don't bother me I'm eatin'!"

"It's got Thiamin!" Bill points at the back label.

"You just cover while I get this in the house, okay?" Mike asks while looking up in thought.

"Can you imagine this with chocolate milk, bro?" Bill asks.

"We're on our way!" Each brother kicks up a heel, and they're off.

Start with Those Around You

"What's next on the list, brother?"

"Milk. Err--that is... *chocolate* milk," Mike says with a wink.

"I mean on the Q List--the start list! Stay with me, dude."

"Yes! the Q List! I would definitely say, 'Start with those around you.' Allow me to elaborate!

"Since everyone has infinite dimensions, facets, stories and value; since everyone is a THOU, then that *includes* the person in the elevator, the person in the office adjacent to yours, the sales floor crew, your next appointment, the client on the phone or the person coming in the door right after you.

"It includes the order-taker at the deli counter, the shelf-stocker, the bakers, that dude there that looks like Santa Claus, or that woman there that... *looks like... someone I... went... to... college...*--why don't we speed it up here real quick."

"HA! You're funny, bro!"

"Glad you liked that one." Mike smiles.

"It's everyone around us," Mike continues. "And so, *they* are with whom you start. No need to make any big deal about exactly who, when, or where. If someone like your friend, John, wants to get the ball rolling, I say try smiling at the person you walk by! Go over and say hi to the person in the office you haven't talked to lately.

"Four things will happen:

"First, **you'll feel GREAT!** You absolutely cannot feel ANY other way. We're dealing with a pillar of the universe here and there's no way around it. Seeing people truthfully, and with genuine kindness is undefeated! It puts a spring in your step immediately and a smile on your face. You can't help but feel better about yourself, about them and about the world around you after simply 'being present with the person near you.'

"Second, it gives you **a spark of momentum that carries you forward** into the next moment--the next opportunity! It's a kick on your skateboard or a good push on your bike pedal. Suddenly it becomes that much easier to do it again. And before you know it, you've just nailed ten Q moments before you've made it to the parking lot or hit the office coffee pot!

"Third, you will truly, literally, scientifically, 'quantum physics'-ally have **changed the energy in your life, and in the life of those you have engaged with,** *and* **in the tangible environment your presence is in contact with**. It's all ripples, man. It's wave lengths. Everything is energy and vibrations--right down to the sub-atomic level. It's energy *that moves by way of* vibrations and when we are present with people, when we love those around us, when we live quintessentially, we create positive frequencies that are indeed felt, and that cause real effect on everything around. That palpable energy is contagious and influential. It is encouraging and motivational. Others find themselves following suit by doing the same, *being* the same! Their vibrations start matching yours! It's a chain reaction that has no end.

"Fourth, by starting with those around you, **you increase your confidence in and ability to engage with those you have a bit more hesitancy talking with,** those you might currently be in an I-IT relationship with. You'll develop a sense of readiness and desire to tackle more challenging conversations with whom you want to be in the We-Zone, but may be reluctant to try with right now.

"And let me add," says Mike. "If John or others are on the shyer side, I get it! And even too, if a situation appropriately calls for less interaction, remember--simple *heart-felt awareness* and maybe a smile is ALL it takes. It can truly start and stay right there!"

With that Mike and Bill are all smiles to everyone passing by.

"Great hat, sir. Love that team," says Bill to a young dad pushing past with a cart and a kid.

"Good choice on the ice cream, sir!" Mike follows to a retired fellow. "Chest bump!"

Mike is awkwardly ignored.

Be Transparent

It wasn't long before a crowd had gathered around Mike and Bill. Their smiles were infectious! Everyone was laughing and exchanging numbers. The highlight though had to be when Bill did a backflip off the laced-together fingers of of a guy named Chris. He nailed it! The clapping and hollering could be heard from the furthest aisle.

"This is livin'!" says Bill as everyone waves goodbye to one another, claps hands and carries on with their shopping.

"Most quintessentially, brother!" says Mike, satisfactorily. "Oh, and hey, --can you read this next word, 'cuz I can't make it out," he asks while pointing to the word with a smirk.

"Veg--eh--tuh--bul--sooop… Nope. Never heard of veg-eh-tuh--something or other. Is it for anything specific do you think?" Bill smirks back.

"Hmmm. Let's see--they did say something about dinner before we left, but… no real specifics on the list. What should we do?

"Well, if it's dinner we need to worry about, then that's easy!" Bill exclaims, as he's off in a flash. Seconds later he's back with a handful of thin boxes. "This is dinner for the dreamers, man!" He says, while dumping them into the cart.

Mike reads, "4 meat, 3 cheese, premium quality, super-duper nutritious, Reddish Baroness PIZZA!!" They both do the shimmy that Janea just taught them back on aisle five.

"You're a genius!" Mike nods, now staring for a long while at the cool picture on the box. We have got to get this in our tummies!

And you've brought over enough, right? In case we need more for dinner tomorrow?"

"I figured nine boxes should do it. Is that not enough?"

"Uh... we better round that up. Go grab three more--just to be safe. You know--make it an even dozen."

Bill comes back and says to Mike, while topping off their leaning tower of pizzas, "Hey--here's one: what about offices that get trained on your Quintessentialism stuff, or a family that's all read the same book? They *all* know about '*Living in the Q*.' Wouldn't that make it awkward to go over to someone the next day and say, "Hey, Bob--just thought I'd come over and say 'hi.' Oh, no real particular reason. Nice tie there though, pal! And I like the neck shave. Haven't really noticed how good you are at that before."

"HA! That's funny. But the question couldn't be better! So glad you brought it up. Easy answer--you just be transparent. IF you feel there's a need, in any way, to explain yourself because you feel that someone's 'on to you' or might feel that you are less than sincere, you offer a genuine, transparent disclaimer. Like this:

"'Bob--how's it going, man. I'm just trying to reset for the day, be my best self and figured by saying hi to some guys in the office, I could get a jump on the morning. Did you watch that game last night?'
    Or, what about...
"'Babe, our conversation last night--for some reason--has still got me bent. I'm sorry, but I've got to get back to a better place--get back to the We-Zone. Is now a good time to talk more about it?'
    Or,
"Miguel--do you have a minute? This Q thing has been awesome for me, and I feel you're the one guy I know least in this whole dang

office. What do you think about hitting lunch later and throwing down the 20 questions?"

Or,

"'Kim, I called you in because I'm wondering if we could 'Q it up' for a minute. I think you left work upset yesterday and I'm hoping we can talk it through and get back to that We-Zone with each other as soon as possible. Do you mind sharing and I promise to only listen, until you feel heard?

One more...

"'Jakov, I know you're worried about your review, and yes--you've had some assignments that we're concerned about. This conversation though--in my mind--is about detaching the challenges you're having from you, the person: because Jakov, we see you as so much more than these isolated difficulties. We-Zone, pal! This review is simply a way of helping you get these kinks worked out, as fast as we can. By the way, how did your daughter's first day of school go?"

"I think my favorite phrase in all of that though, Bill, is this one; 'I'm just trying to be a better person.' 'I'm just trying to be my best self.' I mean, who could possibly be offended by anyone who starts out a conversation like that!?

"I remember when I was living in Vegas years ago and mowing my lawn on a sunny Saturday. My next-door neighbors had the garage door up and were grilling and hanging out with friends. Probably four or five of them. We had never met and we'd lived there a long while already! I felt like now was the best time, the most natural time to stop the lawn mower and be cool, ya know, and finally go over and say hi. But I was scared and nervous and totally in the Me-Zone.

"I mustered up the courage, killed the lawnmower, and walked straight over into very real fear, to where they were. When they saw I was coming across to them directly, they took notice and were no doubt waiting to hear what I was about to say. And this was it: 'Hey guys, how are you? Just trying to be a better neighbor and thought I'd come over and say, 'What's up.'

"Thirty minutes later, we were the best of friends! We actually discovered some fascinating similarities we shared with a random college football team. After that, we were always waving when we saw each other. Virtual fist bumps from that day forward!

"I get you, dude," says Bill. And then he continues, "It's like you could say it for anything: 'I'm just trying to be a better boss', 'I'm just trying to be a better sales rep', 'I'm just trying to do my job the best that I can and wanted to send this email'."

"Exactly!" Mike agrees. "When we are real and transparent about our good, quintessential intentions, people respond *quintessentially!*"

"Hey Mike, just trying to be a better brother. It's time to confess. I was kinda, ...secretly... going out with that girl you had the hots for in high school."

Pay Attention to the Interruptions

"Let's see, how did they forget chips and pop and ice cream on this list?" asks Mike as he looks it over. "They must've been distracted."

"Well, that's what I love about this whole marriage thing. We're here to help each other: complete one another." Bill says, as he ponderously rubs his goatee.

"Complete. I like that word." says Mike. "Chips and salsa complete- -No wait, chips and *queso* complete!

"So, ready for the next 'John bullet point'?" asks Mike.

"Uh… does Billy buy beef?" Bill inquires with a smile, holding up a beef stick and box of crackers.

"Man, you've never lost a step. Now on to our number four: all about paying close attention to the interruptions in our lives, because that's where it's often easiest to miss opportunities to be our quintessential selves.

"Of course, skipping and smiling and finding our groove is always easiest when we're tracking according to plan, or according to our expectations of the day. We might feel the schedule is running smooth and appointments are all falling into place. Maybe it's been an early morning of packing and loading, but now that you've got some miles behind you, the family is happy, and when it comes to your vacation destination, the station wagon is leading the way. You're listening attentively to your wife and children. Life is good in the Q.

"Until it isn't.

"Life has a way of stretching our muscles and working us out, and interruptions are barbells and dumbbells when it comes to living quintessentially.

"I'm borrowing a beautiful phrase and replacing one word with my own when I say: '[Being quintessential] most often happens when we are on the way to something else.'[13]

---

[13] Speech by Kurt R. Saville, *Living a Life of Service and Love: What Goes Around Comes Around* Aug. 1, 2017

"I have found that to be true in my life. Changing plans is often what it's all about to *be* Q and to *stay* in the Q.

"My best example comes from a few years ago when Mom had my name for Christmas and bought me the awesomest Christmas present EVER!"

"Superman Underoos!?"

"Okay, besides that. She bought me the Lego Millennium Falcon with like 1,400 pieces! I was a thirty-something-year-old KID! I couldn't wait to put that together.

"I remember it so clearly. Holiday break. Off work for a while. I'd waited patiently. My kids seemed well contented and pleasantly occupied with their own loot. Distracted! Now, in this quiet stillness was the time! Yes, *now* was the time I had looked forward to for a 'millennium.' I ecstatically wiped off the table real nice, opened my box carefully and began delicately sorting my crinkly clear packages of tiny plastic delights! I was in the Q! Present with those I was with: Han Solo, Chewbacca, Princess Leia *and me!*

"'What could possibly shatter this euphoric solitude?' I thought to myself.

"I shouldn't have asked, 'cause then it happened…

"Like only a monstrous oversized Millennium Falcon destroyer could --complete with googly eyes, chomping teeth, clutching tentacles and grubby hands--my toddler A.J., was on the loose! And he had found me!

"And people were dying!

"And Dad was crying,...

"Wondering, 'Where is your mother!?'

. . . .

"Bill--it had happened. It had come. This was my moment. This was my unexpected interruption--at what seemed for me--the worst of all possible times. This was when Mike met his mettle and had a decision to make. I could reject this little space invader in my 'Me-Zone, I-IT way', and continue being a father who viewed his son as a disturbance to the Force and was therefore ornery and cranky and Darth Vader-like; or I could do something... something that I'm not always good at doing.

"You know me, brother, and I'm glad you understand that by me sharing this story with you, I am by no means implying that I've got this all figured out.

"But on THIS particular occasion, at this magical time of the year, I can say that I was somehow successful at mustering some strength beyond my own, to set aside my expectations, and to be *with* my son--in the We-Zone.

"We played together. We found different pieces, sorted different ways and stuck Legos together, *together*. In fact, he grabbed my instructions at one point and bent them. Instead of reaching for my lightsaber, the now kinder, more loving Obi-Wan in me found a pen and wrote a note--right there on the flipbook--about our shared togetherness at the kitchen table. A time-capsule for the both of us to look back on through the years.

"I'm not saying it's easy. In fact--I'm actually saying it's hard. But the Q moments we have when we're 'on the way to something else', may just be the sweetest moments of them all. Pay attention to the interruptions. In the lyrics of a timeless song, 'Life is what happens... while you're busy making other plans.'[14] "

"Lego party tonight, brother," says Bill as he looks away, blinking hard, hiding his softer side. "And I just remembered my wife needed some tissues, if we can go to that aisle next."

"You're a crack up.

"But seriously, man. I love that story. It encapsulates what life is about. Slowing it down. Being present, one moment at a time with those around us.

"And add to that," continues Bill, "visualize a Dad and daughter playing catch together, or even two adults sitting on a bench talking. And imagine if you could change the setting they're in, or the background behind them with the snap of your fingers, almost like photographs changing on a screen. First, they're playing in their backyard; then snap--it's a city park, then the beach, then the school, then the mountains. Or what if it's two people visiting at a bus stop in a giant city, or now--suddenly at a cafe in Paris, now in Rome, now on a front porch. When you are absolutely in the moment with the person you're with, it's almost like the setting becomes interchangeable, or completely irrelevant. What IS important is the *connection* between those people in the frame. That closeness and sense of presence can make any setting magical, unforgettable, a cinematic masterpiece!"

"I love it! Wow! A *majestic* grocery store aisle this has now become, thanks to you--my brother, Bill!" Mike says with a smile, followed by a very mindful pause between the two of them.

---

[14] quote from song by John Lennon & originally from Allen Saunders, *Reader's Digest*, 1957

"I don't know, should we hug, do you think? Or...?" asks Bill, just as a woman walks by, with a 'I-heard-that' smile.

Count the Q's

"Tissues, check. Your travel size bubble bath, check. I think we're ready for checkout!" Mike says exuberantly. "And with just enough time to give you my last tip for John: I saved my favorite tip for last!"

"Yes! I bet I know this one: 'Tell the wife we no longer need to go on vacations!'"

"HA! I think only Ryan Gosling could pull that off. Actually, it's what I call 'Counting the Q's' and to me it's the way we stay grounded and focused and *centered* in our efforts to live quintessentially. We stand on solid footing inside the Q when doing this. And here's what I mean:

"Bill, we count and measure and keep track of many things in this world and in our lives. We count our money, we count our years, we count our square footage, our gas mileage, our steps, our calories, our followers, our posts, our 'friends' and our 'likes.' We keep track of our vacation days, our waistlines, our clients, our gigs, our appointments, our companies' growth, our teams, the spreads, the scores, the stats, the wins. We count the places we've been, the miles we've run, the things we've done, the toys we have, the things we own...

"And don't misunderstand me, to various degrees and to a certain extent, these countable things bring value and protection, meaning, and happiness to our lives. Some of them are downright crucial and necessary.

"But the *quintessence of our lives* is not found in those lists. The 'most perfect embodiment' of you and me, doesn't come from any of those. The 'essence of' you and me 'in our purest form' is measured differently.

"Our best selves can only be measured by *how often* we find ourselves living quintessentially, by *how often* we are successful at '*living in the Q.*"

"You see Bill, because our best selves blossom, or actualize, or 'become a thing,' or *happen* when we are fully <u>present</u> with the <u>one we are with</u>, then what we should be counting--independent of everything else--are the number of times in our lives when we are doing *just that*.

"A couple things to keep in mind:
"We already know that the *results*, or the effects of being in the Q, are immeasurable. The potential and power for good that come from even one moment that we are there...are infinite.

"Even YOU at that precise moment, being present with your co-worker, friend, wife, child, or the grocery store attendant--maxes you out! It happens in two ways:

"First, you are as amazing in that particular moment as you could possibly be! Even if you were wearing the title of doctor, philanthropist, or Superman, it wouldn't change the level to which you maximized the moment. With a downward swing of the carnival hammer, you've absolutely 'rung the bell' of your 'present potential'!

"And when it comes to fulfilling the one 'universal purpose' that every human being has in common with every other--that of being present with the one they're with--you knock down every bottle with a single throw! What more could you have done in *that* moment, with *that* person? To clarify this point, imagine that you planned an entire year to raise money for and to complete a remarkable charitable event. If that's the case, then allow me to say thank-you right here and now for the difference you're making in the lives of so many, for the number of starfishes you're throwing back. It's noble, remarkable, admirable and appreciated. Your efforts count tremendously. They're simply counted, however... on a separate spreadsheet.

On the Quintessentialism spreadsheet, being present with those you're with *counts just as much* for 'you, the planner' of the event, as it counts for 'you the participant' at the event, as it counts for 'you the recipient' at the event. The bottles you can knock down in each moment are the same. And the potential you've reached in that moment--that precise and beautiful and never-to-come-again moment--is unsurpassable!

"So, the question once again Bill, becomes THIS: How often can we be in the Q: fully present with people? How often can we ring that bell? And how many times can we knock those bottles down?"

"Someone hand me a sledgehammer!" Bill says while looking around at those standing in line with him at checkout. "Anyone got a sledgehammer, handy?!"

Mike laughs. "*That* is 'counting the Q,' brother, and here's what keeping track of your quintessential awesomeness does. And tell John, by the way, that these are simply reinforcing what I mention in chapter 3.

Counting the Q's becomes an incredibly consistent **reminder of what is most important, and what counts the most** among the vast and varied situations and circumstances of our lives. This is our individual and collective END--this is our individual and collective WHY--to be our very best selves, to truly reach our potential and fulfill our purpose. There is nothing that scores higher, or counts more than this.

Counting the Q's is giving yourself a fist bump and a high five on an awesomely consistent basis! It's a **regularly achievable confidence booster and an incredibly satisfying reward** for doing the little things, that really are the big things. You'll be whistling more, singing more, and dancing more on your way to the next place that needs you! Why? Because you've got that Q thang goin' ON, that's why! *Living in the Q* is where you excel, by golly! You're up to 16 Q's and it's not even lunch time!

Counting the Q's **brings a calm and peace to the furious winds and waves of our hectic every day**. Life slows down to the individual moments as they come and go. Life slows down to the individual people we are with, as they also come and go in and out of our lives. Running late for a wedding, or a "Honey--where's my super suit!?" situation, somehow becomes a beautiful beaded chain of moments, like straightening a bowtie for one, and zipping up a dress for another. You sense that being present with those within your reach can happen for you while *planning* for a wedding, *running* to a wedding, as well as *crying* or *dancing* at a wedding. All Q's count the same, and life's moments can count the same as well.

Counting the Q's brings **a deeper sense of purpose and meaning to** what we may otherwise see as **the uneventful, less opportunistic, and less glittery moments or circumstances of life**. Like living through the various stages of a wedding, living through the various stages of our unique conditions in life become more acceptable and more equitable. Our canvases are different, but the opportunities to work with what we're given are the same! The desires are less about wishing or wanting for things to be different, and more about making the most of what we have. We play it like a video game--making the best of the seemingly mundane situation we're in, adventurously, purposefully.

Counting the Q's includes those **calendaring moments when we write in, or block out quintessential time for those extra-special people in our lives.** These Q's count too.

· · · ·

Mike stops talking and notices that the cashier and others behind them are standing quietly, waiting for the next word. Bill and Mike start to laugh as someone jumps in to say, "So can I get all that wisdom on the snack aisle?"

Another says, "It looks like they bought the snack aisle!"

Mike and Bill exclaim, "This IS the snack aisle!"

Everyone laughs as the cashier scans the last item and then asks, "Will this be cash or charge?"

Immediately Bill jumps in to say, "Bro, let me get this. I'm excited to be here and it's the least I can do."

"Thanks pal," Mike responds. "It's a good thing because I'm just noticing that I must have left my wallet on the kitchen table."

Bill's eyes grow saucer size and he turns to Mike with his mouth wide open before he says, "Dude--my wallet's in my suitcase at your house!"

CHAPTER 9
Living in the Q--One is Enough

Today Let's Teleport!

"Hey sweetheart, how busy are you right now?" asks Mike with a projected voice, in hopes of being heard in the other room.

"Oh, I don't know," Lisa says, as she comes into the kitchen holding a paint brush to find Mike staring at his laptop screen. "I'm working on a couple signs that need to be shipped tomorrow,[15] and then the kids get home in a couple hours, but I'm okay. What's up?"

Mike sits back in his chair, turns to Lisa, and says, "I've come to one of the last chapters in my book, and since about the half way point I've been wondering about the perfect way to wrap it all up. Well...it suddenly came to me just now: I know how I want it to end!

"I want *you* to be with me as I talk about what--to me--is the greatest lesson I have ever learned in my life."

"Oh my gosh! What do you need me to do? I'm not sure I can help you out, bud."

"You totally can. All I need you to do is listen. I believe that this will be more easily explained if I'm talking it through conversationally, and there's nobody else I want to do that with in

---

[15] www.42ndCircleDesign.etsy.com

the whole world, more than you. You've lived so much of this with me. Oh,...and we'll need to teleport."

"What!? Teleport? What are you talking about?" Looking puzzled, Lisa crinkles her eyebrows.

"It's *my* book! I get to write it however I choose and I know where I want to take you. I mean, who wants to read a book about two people talking in the kitchen? Dream big, is what I say! We'll snap our fingers and we're there!"

"Oh, this is funny, Mike."

"I promise, we'll be back before the kids come home," Mike says reassuringly.

"So, where are we going?"

"I want to surprise you, but you'll love it! All you need to do is have a seat right here, hold my hand, and we're off." Mike pulls another kitchen chair closer to his and motions for her to sit.

"Well, if it's because of your book..." says Lisa, "And could we possibly have a clean house by the time we get back?"

"With cookies in the oven, babe!"

. . . .

In a blink, Mike and Lisa find themselves sitting on a newly painted, beautiful park bench on a gorgeous spring day. Their bench is near the edge of, and facing, a circular roundabout with immaculate streets and curbs, flowers and green grass all around. From the roundabout center, people with smiles walk happily in the direction the curvy streets take them. Some are headed north, others south, and others east and west.

Mike and Lisa are facing a towering, moving orbital mobile of golden spheres and planetary globes, with rockets of people soaring right above them! Just behind and to the left is the iconic Matterhorn and further left is the beautiful Sleeping Beauty's Castle.

"You teleported us to Disneyland!?" Lisa figures out after a couple blinks of her now wide eyes.

"How can you tell?" Mike smiles. "I know we haven't been here much, but the last time was so memorable for me, and I recall thinking several times that it sure would be neat to be here together, just the two of us. I can't imagine a cooler date. I've had it in my mind ever since, and when I was thinking about a place to end my book, I knew when I thought it, that this was the place!"

"Uh... well, THIS WORKS! Can you write a book *every* day?"

"Absolutely! Let's call the next one *Mike and Lisa Go to Space--at Disneyland!*" smiles Mike.

Lisa responds with, "And the next will be, *Mike and Lisa Ride the Rails...*"

"*At Disneyland!*" they both laughingly say together!

"We're getting the hang of this!" Mike rubs his hands together.

A Lifetime Lesson

"Alright," Lisa says, slowing things down a bit. "We're here so you can talk, and I can listen. Where do you want to start?"

"Thanks, babe. I think I want to start by explaining that some lessons aren't always learned from a book, or in a day. Some lessons can take years, even a *lifetime*, and the last lesson for this book is one of those. It is the most important lesson I have learned, and it's taken my life to learn it."

"I think I know what you want to share." Lisa smiles. "But, let's hear your version."

Mike begins with a smile and a sigh. "So, as you know... I had a pretty amazing childhood. I remember being happy. I was a blonde-haired, optimistic boy that loved life. It didn't matter that financially things were tight. In terms of fond memories growing up, I am a rich man! My mind is packed with cheerful and untroubled images of playing in the neighborhood, being carefree and enjoying the wonders of learning and life--especially during my grade school years. I loved my teachers and my classmates. It is all so vivid in my mind. (And sheesh!--Now I can't even remember last week!)

"Or the names of our kids," Lisa reminds him with a smile.

"We still have four, right?" Mike smiles back. "Anyway, I also remember lots of compliments from my teachers and other adults in my life, awards and accomplishments that were very meaningful. Seriously, sweetheart, I think I peaked in elementary school." Mike chuckles to himself.

"All of this had a very interesting effect on me. First, I looked forward to the future. I saw a million possibilities for my life, and my confidence in being exactly who I wanted to be--of who I dreamed I could be--was as big as," Mike pauses for just the right comparison, "as big as Disneyland on a day like this!

"But then... life happens, I guess you could say, and no matter how hard I thought I tried--after many years--it didn't seem to be the way I imagined. Which leads me to the second effect that my upbringing has had on me: I often looked back on my life with questions. I was troubled by the thought that somehow, I wasn't as successful as I could've been.

"I think people can relate, sweetheart," says Lisa as she holds his hand a little tighter. "I know a lot of people, who feel that way, and surely you've met some. While we are young, the world is full of possibilities and as we continue down the path life takes us and see the results of our choices, we don't always end up where we thought we would."

"How did I miss Pixar's initial public stock offering?!" questions Mike with a wink and a grin. Lisa hits Mike's leg with his hand she's holding. They both look up to take in the sites of the 'Happiest Place on Earth.' Even the pigeons look happy as they peck the grass around the bench where Lisa and Mike are sitting.

When Life's A Little Less...

"Hey!" Mike says as he slaps his knee. "We need *tasty* at a time like this! You know--talking about all the 'what-might've-beens.' Why don't we have some ice cream while we're chatting? Ooh! That famous Pineapple Dole Whip! Sound good to you?"

"I'm okay, babe. Besides, I'm liking where we are, and don't want to lose this great seat."

"Ah, my dear--how quickly you forget!" Mike snaps his fingers and instantly Donald and Daisy Duck are handing them each a Dole Whip! In amazement, Mike and Lisa set their cups down on the bench and give each of their new fluffy friends a big hug! Although in no rush to leave, but after plenty of waves and smiles, the two feathery lovebirds bounce along their merry way.

Sitting back down, Lisa inquires, "Uh… how did you pay for this babe?"

"Oh gosh. I told Mickey to put it on my tab," he laughs with a spoon in his mouth. They both smile.

. . . .

"So, like many," Lisa says to return to the topic, "you've come to learn, that despite hard work and daily efforts, our paths of life often take turns we hadn't planned, wrote about, or colored pictures of when we were young. And to many, this means they haven't been successful; maybe even sometimes to you."

"Precisely. And that can lead to therapy sessions!" Mike cracks himself up, laughing loud enough that passersby turn to see what's funny.

"If we're not careful," explains Mike, "the questions we start asking ourselves can look and sound like, 'Where did *I go wrong?*' or, 'How did *I miss* the success that I thought was waiting for me?' As it often goes, a gap begins to widen between life's expectations and life's realities. And the wider the gap--as months turn into years--the greater the need to *explain* it and the more we look for the reasons that caused it. And unfortunately, the first go-to for most is **to negatively reflect on <u>ourselves</u>.**

"Yes," he continues, "we are responsible for the things we can control, and yes, some better decisions could've closed the gap, but there is also a glaring explanation that many of us miss. A reason that is seldom mentioned and even less understood--less felt, less acknowledged!

"We miss what's *most* important. *I* missed what's most important. And it's this overlooked reality that helped me, and can help all of us--close the gap!"

"Well babe! I know we've talked together about life many times, but I can't remember talking about a missed explanation for these gaps between what we thought would happen and what did happen. I'm very curious to know what that is!

Mike leans forward and looks around for a couple of moments. They see the strollers, the group selfies, the kids being hurried along by longer arms. After Mike scrapes a couple small Dole Whip bites from the side of his cup, Lisa impatiently exclaims, "Enough waiting already! What did we miss?"

Success Defined

With that, Mike's 'Mickey Mouse train of thought' starts on to the next station. **"We miss accurate _definitions_ of success.**

"More than our _inadequacies_, our definitions for words like '_success_,' '_accomplished_,' '_great_' and '_important_' need to be a topic equally addressed when discussing the gaps in our lives. Much of the discrepancy between what we thought meant 'life well lived,' and what actually occurred, comes from an inaccurate perception of what 'life well lived' really entails.

"When we understand this, that gap closes, and life is no longer the missed opportunity we thought! We find that we were always closer to success than we believe, are closer now than ever, and can even be successful ever after--in practically _every_ moment!

. . . .

The best definition I have found for 'success' comes from someone I knew so little about, but have come to appreciate so very much. His name is Dag Hammarskjöld. Wikipedia states that:

"[He] was a Swedish economist and diplomat who served as the 2nd Secretary-General of the United Nations. [He] was the youngest person to have held the post, at an age of 47 years.... His second term was cut short when he was killed in an airplane crash... [He was 56 years old.] He is one of only four people to be awarded a posthumous Nobel Prize." [16]

---

[16] https://en.wikipedia.org/wiki/Dag_Hammarskjöld

I also found this: "Immediately following [his appointment], Hammarskjöld attempted to establish a good rapport with his staff. He made a point in going to every UN department to shake hands with as many workers as possible, eating in the cafeteria as often as possible, and relinquishing [his] private elevator for general use."

Lastly, I learned that President John F. Kennedy said of Mr. Hammarskjöld at his passing, "I realize now that in comparison to him, I am a small man. He was the greatest statesman of our century."

And here, finally, is the quote attributed to him. I love it so.

**"It is more noble
to give yourself completely to one individual,
than to labor diligently for the salvation of the masses."**

"Yes! I remember that--it's close to your heart," says Lisa. "I'm glad you're including him and his quote in your book."

"His words are the best summary I have of my 'life's lesson,' sweetheart, my greatest truth about the expectation gap I've sometimes had in my life. In his words is the definition for life's most important achievement, and how it happens.

"One Individual"

"First--as Mr. Hammarskjöld makes clear--**life is about living for the ONE**. The famous Russian author of *War and Peace,* Leo Tolstoy, declared, "The most important person is the one you are with in this moment." I think that is exactly what Dag is saying. If I may use a little literary license--with Mr. Hammarskjöld's blessing of course--this is how I'd alter his quote, as if he were speaking just to me.

"'Mike, it is more noble to give yourself completely to [*the*] one [*you are with*] than to [*write a book for the masses* about giving yourself completely to the one you are with].'

"'It is more noble to be kind to the one, than to give a noble speech about being kind to the one.'

"'It is more noble to be patient with the one, than to have noble meetings about being patient with the one.'

"'It is more noble to throw back the starfish nearest you, than to create a noble program to help others throw back the starfish nearest them.'

"That makes so much sense, Mike," says Lisa. "I mean, blogging, posting, tweeting or even talking about the nobleness of being with your family, will never be the same as actually turning off the 'noise of life' and being with your family.

"The END is the *one!*" says Lisa, as she reflects upon the conversation. "That is 'success,' and being 'accomplished,' and 'important!' And too, when we think about those people in our lives, that we admire most, that we would give honorary 'Dag Hammarskjöld' or 'Q Awards' to, who would they be?"

"They'd be those that very few people on this planet even know," answers Mike. "They'd be those that didn't always fit today's definition or perception of 'success.' To them, those mainstream definitions mattered not at all."

"You're right," agrees Lisa. "They are the ones that found life's purpose in those *one-on-one* relationships they were blessed to have around them. Their life's focus on the one, *became* their life's success!"

In the Q 'Completely'

"Sweetheart, how would you like some Minnie Mouse ears, while we're enjoying this time together, sitting here on a park bench at Disneyland?"

"Oh, no need. But thanks. Happy to just be here. It's so amazing!" replies Lisa.

"Are you suuure you don't want Minnie Mouse ears?" asks Mike, as he smiles and stares directly at the top of her head.

"Yes. I'm sur -" she suddenly stops, and then with both hands reaches up to the top of her head to feel felt Minnie Mouse ears with a big red and white polka-dotted hair bow in the middle! "Mike! How long have those been there!" she squeaks.

"What about gloves--would you like some white -"

"AHHH! Okay--get them off right now!" Lisa screams as she pulls down her arms to see giant gloves on her hands.

"And shoes! I think you'd look good with -"

"Okay, this is NOT funny!" Now her giant Minnie Mouse stilettos are about to trip pedestrians.

Mike is laughing so hard, tears stream down his cheeks, though no sound can be heard. He's holding his sides all the while Lisa is saying, "I am leaving right now if these don't disappear, Mister! One, two..."

Before she gets to four, Mike waves the hand that isn't holding his side and they instantly disappear. "C'mon babe," between gasps, "Have a little fun."

"Uh... that isn't fun, and just wait--when I write *my* book, I'll turn you into a frog!"

Mike dries his eyes, "Okay, princess." They sit together a moment watching a man holding what seemed to be a hundred balloons walking by. There were people everywhere, all with delightful intentions. Wonderful places to go. Magical places to be.

"I think there's something very interesting about the word 'completely' that Mr. Hammarskjöld chooses to use in his quote.

My second gem comes from looking at this word's two beautiful facets.

"One side of this jewel of a word 'completely' comes from the meaning that's been implied as we've been talking just now, about being completely present **in the moment.** 'It is more noble to give yourself completely **[in the moment!]** to one individual...' Dag understood that life is a chain of moment to moment interactions with individuals. He understood--to use Q language--that 'being *fully present*, **in the moment** with the one you are with' is living at possibly the noblest of levels. (At the quintessential level!)

"But the word 'completely' could also imply a *duration*: a span, even a lifetime! Listen to his quote now, with this new meaning attached: 'It is more noble to give yourself completely **[throughout a lifetime]** to one individual than to labor diligently for the salvation of the masses.'

"Sweetheart, I believe Mr. Hammarskjöld knew this too, that if in our lives, **all we HAD was *one*--to whom we truly gave ourselves completely--it would be noble. And even more, it would be *enough!*** The many--or the masses--are what we typically have available, as we go about our lives, but even IF it's one... it's all that is called for, for us to be our very best selves. One is all that the 'quintessential equation' needs. One is sufficient. One allows us to be transformed quintessentially. One other person, **[throughout a lifetime]** fused together with us in that We-Zone, I-THOU way, is all that's REQUIRED for you and I to be in each moment, the very best you and me that we could ever possibly be!

"And *that* is the definition of greatness. Being our best selves, by '*living in the Q*' where <u>Presence</u> meets <u>Humanity</u> *is* achievement, it is accomplishment... it is success!"

"What a soul-satisfying realization, Lisa responds. "And! --It's *the* definition that gives every MOMENT of our lives an equal opportunity for us to *be* successful and to *live* successfully!

. . . .

"I think before you end your book," says Lisa, "You should tell the story about our son, and the conversation you had with him a while ago. I think it would illustrate just how true all of this is."

"You think so? Okay, but just as long as everybody reading this knows, that I am not one to score very high on the 'presence with people' graph at all, as surprising as that might be to some. I feel like I'm such a scatterbrain, who can hardly focus most of the time. You tell them, babe! This whole Quintessentialism thing is for me most of all. Remember, I didn't choose this book, it chose me!"

"I'm sure they understand. You are human, and life is a process. One day at a time, babe."

"Well, okay. Here we go. One day you related something that happened at school, involving our son, that a teacher had mentioned to you. He was in elementary school and had just been in the wrong place at the wrong time. We thought it was a perfect time to reinforce the importance of respecting others.

"That afternoon, Jake and I happened to be on some bleachers, watching his little brother at a T-ball game. I mentioned that his teacher had called, and to tell me what happened. He told me briefly about the mix-up.

"I then asked Jake to think of someone in his class that he admired, and looked up to. I wanted him to name an individual that I could then use as an example to say, 'Jake, the way you see so-and-so, is the way many others see you. People look up to you. People are watching you, buddy.'

"Well, after asking him the question, he just sat silently and didn't say a thing. The pause was surprising. How hard is it to think of someone in your class that you think is cool? I started to wonder if he hadn't completely understood the question. I tried rephrasing it, using more general terms.

"Still, no answer. I was even more confused. 'Bud,' I said, 'who, then, in the entire grade, do you look up to, or like, or want to be like, or see as a role model.' I thought by widening the pool of candidates we'd speed this up a bit.

"Again, no answer. Just silence. Alright. Now it became, 'Who in the whole school, or neighborhood, or in the city, do you admire, and want to be like?' 'How hard is this question?' I kept thinking to myself. A quick answer is all I needed: this wasn't a term paper.

"And then he said something I will never forget for as long as I live.

"My 11-year-old son, said, 'Dad, it's *you*.'

"I was speechless. It surprised me as much as anyone could be surprised. I wouldn't have seen that coming in a million years.

"Sweetheart," Mike says as he pauses for a moment, looks up at the Matterhorn, and then over at Lisa. "We started this last chapter with me wanting to share what has been for me, the greatest lesson I've ever learned. This story illustrates what I've come to know. I have come to understand that on the 'Scale of Compliments,' or on the 'Scale of Success,' or 'Achievement', or 'Importance'… my son, Jake's, three little words, 'Dad, it's you' outweigh the world.

"It is more noble to [receive a compliment from your *son*, who wants to be like you] than to [receive countless compliments from] the masses."

Lisa holds Mike's hand. "It's a great story. And he's got a great, not-always distracted Dad," she says with a wink.

"You know what?" Mike says, as he stretches out his legs and wipes his eyes discreetly. "I've wondered and thought for a while now about how I would respond if someone were to ask me, "So what actually IS the phrase or motto, or written answer that explains the life lesson you've learned?'

"Guess what? I found it while being on this park bench with you:

"The *most* important kind of success, and the *most* important kind of achievement happens between you--and *one* other."

"By living quintessentially, we do that! Before lunch, after lunch, and every moment in between.

. . . .

"Thanks for listening and chatting here with me, babe. It's turned out to be exactly as I hoped." says Mike as he straightens his shirt and then smiles at his wife. "Should we hit a ride before we get back to the clean house--and fresh cookies?"

"YES! I'm thinking Star Tours! It's always been one of my favorites.

"Done! Should we get Aladdin to fly us over on the carpet?"

"Uh... don't you DARE! I actually would prefer walking. Joy in the journey. Being present with the one I'm with," smiles Lisa. "And not freaking out about falling off!"

Mike and Lisa hold hands and begin walking away. "I'm afraid I've got a sappy movie line for you, that I know you're not going to like."

"Oh no. Be careful."

"I love *living in the Q* with you!"

"UUGH! Puhleez!" she replies with a laugh.

[*Camera pans back, and up... see the crowd, now the park... Mike and Lisa stay center... now fireworks, cue Tinkerbell... blue sky with clouds... and cut!*] "That's a wrap, everybody!

Section Two:

THE ADDENDUM FOR WORK AND LIFE

CHAPTER 1
Q Companies! — Work Problems Solved Quintessentially!

"Don't You Know who I Am!?"

"Are you Mike Forsyth?"

"Yes. I am."

"Hi. I'm Ann. The CEO will see you now. Right this way. How are you liking New York City today?"

"Thank you so much, Ann. Oh, very lovely. Especially from way up here. Wow! Oh, here's his office. Great. Thanks again and so nice to meet you, Ann."

"Come in and shut the door! Have a seat!" a voice shouts from inside the room.

Mike goes in, shuts the door, and takes a seat.

"You've got a lot of nerve being here right now. I mean, you do know who I am, don't you!? I don't accept many sales calls so this better be good."

"Uh... yes, sir. I know who you are. You are Mr. Ebenezer--"

"Call me 'Mr. Sir'! Haven't you seen the movie *Holes*!? 'Mr. Sir' will do just fine."

"Yes sir, Mr. Sir. So... to answer your question, you are Mr. Sir and you are the CEO of a big company that--"

"That's enough! And you are correct. It's a super duper big, big, BIG company! And we make a LOT of money! And I am very important and extremely RICH! And I am extremely to the point! I cut right down to the brass tacks and I mean business, by golly! You know that scene in the movie *Top Gun* where the Sergeant at the beginning is yelling right in front of Tom Cruise's face!?
"Uh...yes."

"Do you remember the part where he says, 'Your ego's writing checks your body can't cash'!?"

"Yes, I do."

"THAT'S ME!" He yells loudly and slaps his hands on his desk. "Have you ever seen *Spiderman*, the first movie...and I think the second one too, and maybe the third? The Newspaper boss guy?" Mike nods.
"THAT'S ME TOO!"

We both look at each other for a second, in silence. Then Mr. Sir speaks again, pacing to the window.

"Your face, Mike, is all over the dang place these days. You're on billboards, throwing out first pitches. Sheesh, I even saw you dancing with some band on T.V. the other night. You've got two minutes to tell me why you're such a big deal, why I should be talking to you, and why my company needs you, or by hell or high-water Mike Forsyth, you're walking the plank! You ever seen a pirate movie with a guy in it like me before? That's RIGHT you haven't cuz THERE AIN'T ONE!! Captain Hook and Davy Jones got nothin' on me! Now get talking before I throw you OUTTA HERE like that umpire did as he was yelling at that baseball manager on T.V. not too long ago! <u>PROCEED</u>!"

The Quintessential Close

With that, Mike stands up and squares his shoulders and checks that his tie is nice and straight. He's got a slightly noticeable smile and a twinkle in his eye. He seems relaxed, confident, poised. He begins.

"Mr. Sir, I believe you would agree that relationships are pivotal, if not the most critical, component of success in work and personal life. Correct?"

Mr. Sir nods.

"Wonderful. I personally believe that **relationships are everything.** To me, our success in work and life begins and ends with the quality of our relationships. When our relationships are healthy and thriving, we can't be happier. I mean, we could have all the money in the world and be lonely or fighting with someone and it would be a miserable day. Would you agree?"

"Completely."

"Excellent. Guess what, Mr. Sir? My passion is all about relationships! Improving relationships, both for you and your company. Look at this list on my tablet, Mr. Sir. These are all the many ways that relationships affect your company's success. Every one of these relationships is addressed through my consulting company, and built upon the mental framework of what I call Quintessentialism.

- Customer/Client ↔ Office Manager
- Prospect/Lead ↔ Sales Associate
- Colleague ↔ Colleague
- Employee ↔ Competitor

- Superior ↔ Subordinate
- Team Leader ↔ Team Member
- Business Partner ↔ Organizational Rep
- Employee ↔ Family member or Friend

"If these relationships above are working properly, Mr. Sir, if each of these relationships are vibrant, clicking and running at optimum level, then look at what happens! And this list below?… it's always growing!

- Increased productivity & work efficiency
- Increased collaboration & synergy
- Increased prospect and lead pipelines
- Increased employee health & well-being
- Increased trust, respect, tolerance & civility
- Increased job satisfaction & engagement
- Increased profitability and company growth
- Increased sense of purpose & self esteem

- Decreased hostility, conflict & infighting
- Decreased employee turnover & hiring costs
- Decreased absentee costs
- Decreased behavioral management
- Decreased customer complaints & negative reviews
- Decreased loss of disenchanted client revenue
- Decreased employee escapism, withdrawal & time waste

"Mr. Sir, the reason I can address every one of the relationship pairs I've shown you, and help you achieve the results you see here as well, is because Q-ism addresses the foundational way in which we see each other, the way that we see every other person in our lives. Starting here, at the first step--the first bedrock level--is the key! Fundamental and foundational change *necessitate* that we start with the fundamentals, and at the very foundation!

"I'm listening" said Mr. Sir. "I mean, I'm LISTENING!"

"Mr. Sir, Q-ism is a distillation of years of learning about relationships. I have quite a toolset! I can take it to deeper levels in specific areas by customizing our training around problems that *you* identify! We'll build a game plan of training around these areas of emphasis.

And we'll prescribe concrete next steps for your company--not just offer motivational ideas that are forgotten when I leave. For example, Mr. Sir, looking at this next graphic, can you tell me an

Workplace Problems Addressed by Q-ism	By seeing others as *PEOPLE	We become PRESENT with them	And unlock our *PURPOSE & POTENTIAL	Which compels us to have this PROCESS	Of creating POWERFUL & POSITIVE relationships
Communication	✗	✗	✗	✗	✓
Culture	✗	✗	✗	✗	✓
Customer Care	✗	✗	✗	✗	✓
Diversity	✗	✗	✗		✓
Employee Interaction	✗	✗	✗	✗	✓
Employee Engagement	✗	✗	✗	✗	✓
Internal Conflict	✗	✗	✗		✓
Job Performance	✗	✗	✗	✗	✓
Leadership	✗	✗	✗	✗	✓
Team Dynamics	✗	✗	✗	✗	✓
Work-life Balance	✗	✗	✗	✗	✓

area of concern within your company that you'd like to work on? It's okay sir, you can be honest with me."

"The truth, huh?" responds Mr. Sir.

"Yes, I'd like the truth, Mr. Sir, sir."

"You want the truth!?" he says more loudly.

"Yup, I want the truth."

"You can't handle the 'truth'!" he sneers. "Employee interaction-- that's a good one, employee engagement."

"I'm sorry, Mr. Sir., did you say, employee interaction and engagement?"

"<u>YOU'RE DANG RIGHT I DID!!</u>" he bellows from his desk.

"Got it, Mr. Sir. Thank you," Mike says with a smile. "Now let's look back at the chart.

"Notice how both employee interaction and employee engagement are absolutely applicable to all four areas of my Q-ism Process! We've got you and your company covered, Mr. Sir!

"Mr. Sir, working together, your organization can be free of the countless challenges resulting from poor relationships! You'll be working effectively at the heart of the matter, and building on the foundation from which all change begins. You can be tremendously more influential as an organization because from the ground up, your employees and teams will be more positive, present and powerfully productive. Let's start today to see and be and live… quintessentially!

Mr. Sir stands slowly, all the while looking Mike squarely in the eye. "Do you remember the part in the *Beauty and the Beast*?…not the most recent live action one, but the animated one, where the Beast says to Bell, "And you will join me for dinner!"

"Yes, I do. I like that part," says Mike.

"Well watch this then," as he pushes his phone beeper for Ann up at the reception desk.

"This is Ann."

"Ann," he growls in a low and gruff voice, "You will book Mike for trainings!!

"AND THAT'S NOT A REQUEST!"

CHAPTER 2
"Can I truly See--Quintessentially?"

Quests from Crazy Questions

Oh, the distances we'll travel for an answer to a question! There's absolutely no coincidence to the fact that the word quest is found in the word *quest*ion. Finding the answers to our most compelling questions are powerful motivations in life. They can change the world! Here's a good one: "Can I fit?"

One hot summer day when I was about 14, my little brother and I had somehow found ourselves locked out of our house. No one was home and we were stuck with nothing to do. Mom never locks the front door when she runs errands and why in the world she decided to lock the doors that day, I'll never know. My 7-year-old brother and I did everything we could to find a way in. Checked every window, even rubbed popsicle sticks sharp on one end to stick in the key hole, hoping it would turn the door knob. Nothing turned.

Hot, dry summer kept rolling along for several hours it seemed, and no trace of Mom, and absolutely nothing to do. It was about then that I wondered if it was possible for me to squeeze myself between our brown, wooden front door, and the metal and glass screen door that you find on many of the homes in our neighborhood back then. What a question! It looked possible. If I sucked in and turned my head, I was sure I could do it. I tried to fit on my own a few times, but somehow, I couldn't pull the storm door shut and get it locked tight from the inside: no leverage with my crammed hand and wrist.

"Hey Billy," I shouted! "C'mere bro." Billy came over and I told him of my brilliant plan. I'd be the first in history to do it. Imagine the bragging rights I'd have with my friends! I'd be a living legend. "There goes Mike, the first kid to ever lock himself between a wood door and a screen door and live to tell about it!"

"So here's the plan," I said. "I'll squeeze myself in and when I give you the signal, you push the screen door shut. Make sure you hear it lock. Got that?"

Little Billy looked up with the most trusting, loyal eyes and nodded. I had no doubt he could make it happen.

"And just as important… when I tell you to open the screen door, you've got to do that too, okay?"

Again, a nod that only Lassie could pull off better.

I stepped in. Positioning my feet securely, I pointed my feet away from each other in order to fit. I put my hands up beside my face, and sucked in deeply. I looked at Billy the best I could, face turned sideways, and gave him the signal. Without hesitation, the two chubby little hands pushed the door shut. With a bit of a shove right there toward the end, we heard the door 'click' shut. *I had done it!*

I'd answered the question! My quest to *know* had led me to a successful outcome! I'd climbed the mountain peak, I'd circumnavigated the globe! I had squeezed myself between two doors! YES!

"Can I fit? Yes, I CAN!"

See me basking in my glory. Soaking up the moment. *(pause)* *(pause)* *(pause once more)*

And then it was time to get out.

"Okay pal. Go ahead and open it up." Billy grabbed the handle with both hands, put both little thumbs on the handle's release button and pushed. Can you say, "STUCK?!"

In an instant, we both realized it was not going to budge, and that little Billy's thumbs stood no chance! It was precisely at that same instant little Billy's face melted in horror! I can still see it to this very day. (Think Edvard Munch's painting, 'The Scream'.) I'd wedged in there so tight that the lock was jammed. And he and I had a problem.

"Go get the neighbors!"

And that's the story of how Mike Forsyth got himself stuck in his door, and the neighbors had to come over laughing, with kids, dogs, and everyone, to set him free. *(With considerable force I might add!)*

How an Axiom was Born

This is *also* the long-winded way in which Mike tees up his point that deeply passionate questions lead to lifelong quests, and memorable experiences, and wild rides, and to many places, Mike NEVER thought he'd go!

My quest (okay, back to first person now) continues today, and is already 20 years in the making, as I've been wondering and exploring and searching to understand relationships and human connectivity. And it all started with one personally irrepressible question:

Is it <u>truly</u> possible to live free of troubled emotions in all of my relationships, both at work and at home?

Years of reading, studying, searching, testing and retesting has led me to some wonderful answers! It's also led me on a journey that's created some valuable resources and unique perspectives:

As a lifelong learner, tormented by a quest to find answers to my relationship troubles, **I've been fortunate to find information, strategies, and best practices that have proven themselves**, both for my benefit and for the <u>benefit of so many like me</u>. This information comes from the best books, and to my surprise, often from the least recognized sources.

As a professional, lifelong teacher, and business professional, I have found myself wanting to **distill the answers I've discovered into simple, packageable gems, ready for application in meaningful ways and within any environment.** I love to sort, compartmentalize and organize ideas, making the information as orderly, sensible, logical, approachable, and useful as possible!

I've learned that philosophers and others don't often write for you and me, but for distinguished colleagues, and their efforts to bring principles of learning to our level can be difficult. Yet, often times the best information is the hardest to explain. One of my favorite books, for example, I've read over four times. The last time I immersed myself in it was with the specific intent of formulating the gems inside into capsules of useable information for all people. **<u>Quintessentialism was born through this process!</u>**

My passion in life is to **share my key learnings and personal experiences with individuals and organizations everywhere**. I help in ways and perspectives yet to be attempted by others. My aim is to help people to be their best selves, their quintessential selves, as often as humanly possible.

And to think, all that from a question! "Hey, hold my drink. I wonder if I can…"

For more information about living free from troubled relationships at both work and home, please find me-- Mike Forsyth--on all social media channels, as well as at my websites: <u>mikeforsyth.com</u> and <u>liveintheq.com</u>. Training in various formats is available. Customizable opportunities are waiting!

The Q Process Visually--Upward and Outward

Being your very best self creates ripples that cannot be contained! As much as you may try, *living in the Q* has profoundly positive effects that you can't get back in the bag! This is because Quintessentialism is an **ever expanding and ascending axiom**. (Okay, a cycle, or process, but I like the ring!)

It begins with a focus on seeing others in a very unique and truthful way – we see them as *people*, and not as things.

By seeing others as PEOPLE
*not things

Seeing others as *people* connects us to them, and also draws them to us. This connectedness, in actuality, is to be fully *present* with them. We are a positively bonded pair.

This sense of being *present* with *people* changes our nature! We **embody interdependent attributes** like care and concern, respect and appreciation, trustworthiness and loyalty. We are, in reality, our *very best* in these moments, we are our "**quintessential**" selves. While in this state of being we actualize our *present potential* and we fulfill our *universal purpose and meaning*. This is the <u>aim</u> and the <u>end</u> for not only every human interaction, but for every human endeavor.

Surprising to many, this state of actualizing our *purpose* and *potential* as we are *present* with *people* **can be frequently achieved**! Therefore, focusing on the *process* of living in such a connected way to others – so as to attain to the best within us, as often as possible – should be **our primary concern**.

Doing "the next right thing," for example, no matter the result, honors process. This is an abundant mindset, as opposed to a paradigm of scarcity and fear.   It is the key to high-trust relationships and breeds greater success in all aspects of work and life.

Individuals and organizations that honor the *process* of being their *very best*, by achieving *presence* with *others*, are **tremendously influential!** They create *powerful relationships* that *positively* transform individuals, environments, and cultures of all sizes! They are change agents and difference-makers. Their impact on individuals and the world is incalculable!

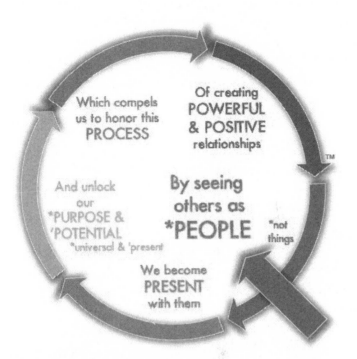

The Quintessentialism Process™
For Powerful & Positive Relationships

A *See to Be* Rock Concert!

Ten thousand people, maybe more[17]--are going nuts! They've been screaming and singing along with their favorite band, R.E.M., all evening, in a surprise reunion and one-night-only flash concert at the local park! The news trucks were all over the place, and plenty of friendly neighborhood law enforcement we're enjoying the moment as well.

Of course, everyone is thinking it's a dream, spending a spontaneous evening with one of the greatest bands of all time, and all. I mean, what band sticks together for thirty years and sells over 85 million copies of their studio albums alone? Exactly! From 1980, they were one of the first alternative bands to hit it 'bigtime', from good ol' Athens, Georgia USA, and they stayed on top for decades, which included a mainstream streak in the late 80's and early 90's when albums *Green, Out of Time, Automatic for the People* and *Monster* topped the charts over and over and over again.

But nobody could prepare the crowd for what happened next! With about three songs left to go on their playlist, Michael Stipe, the

---

[17] Simon and Garfield, *Sound of Silence*

band's lead singer quieted the crowd. Panting a bit, he said, "What a night! We're the luckiest band in the world to have fans like you. We wondered if we'd been forgotten."

The roar was deafening. And two minutes later they settle down to hear what else Michael had to say.

"I've never done this before, but the band and I want to bring out a great fan and friend of ours, and someone that you have absolutely got to meet. We met him a couple years ago when he kept making us all laugh backstage on our world tour. I was like, 'who is this total stud!?' Speaking for all of us, we're not sure we've ever met a more strong, approachable, smart, talented, well-rounded and fascinating guy! But along with that, he's helped us figure out what it means to be our best selves, or to be our quintessential selves. We're now *living in the Q* as often as we can, and we love him for it! Give it up for our buddy and relationship guru--Mike Forsyth!"

With that, the crowd goes bonkers! Huge pyrotechnics blast from the stage, drum rolls echo into the electric air, and guitar riffs give Mike's walk out a mesmerizing moment that maybe (!) Michael Jackson had once in his life. The girls screamed! The guys were totally freaking out!

Mike Forsyth, in his t-shirt and jeans, walks up to Michael and hugs ensue. "Great to be here everybody! R.E.M.--number one!" Mike Forsyth yells into the mic, as the sea of fans flip out again.

"No man," says Michael Stipe. "*You're* number one! So, tell us man...I understand you've got a new training workshop that coincides with your book. Tell us what this *See to Be* training is all about? And more specifically, what does it have to do with Quintessentialism. We want our fans to know."

"Thanks, Michael. I'm grateful for the opportunity. It's a fabulous question. As you know Michael, and as I'm here to share, Quintessentialism is what happens when you cross the pillar of mindfulness, or being present, with the other great pillar of life; loving people and helping others. What is born from that collision is the axiom to *'Live in the Q,' 'Love in the Now,' 'Be Present with People,'* and to *'Be Mindful of Mankind'*.

"To truly achieve this axiom, however, it requires that you see others around you as people, and not as things, or objects. That can be easier said than done! It's very hard to do with our troubled relationships--you know, the people in our lives that we're not in the optimum place with right now. My *See to Be* training specifically addresses that challenge, and teaches people key concepts and strategies to see others truthfully, as people, like themselves. This is the key to unlocking real change in these relationships. It's the key to *living in the Q* with absolutely everyone!

"It's organized into four key areas that I've created through years of study. Each area focuses on transforming people by helping them see others truthfully, or better yet... quintessentially!"

"Is that crazy or what!?" yells Michael Stipe. The crowd roars in approval, as if it's what they've always wanted and knew they needed, but just didn't know where to find it.

"So, what are the four categories?" asks Michael.

"I'm glad you asked! The four categories are:
See the Signs,
See thy Self,
See their Story, and
See to Serve."

And with that, giant images of Mike's four iconic symbols are projected onto some huge screens made from massive fabrics held up by cranes behind the stage. The icons twirl and expand. Peter Buck, the lead guitarist, lays down some seriously twirly riffs. The crowd can't believe it.

Mike Forsyth, while looking over his shoulder, pointing and speaking a lot louder says, "Each category includes a collection and distillation of proven insights found in the best books about overcoming the Me-Zone we can find ourselves stuck in. It also includes to-do lists, action items and next steps to help people and organizations achieve breakthroughs in their relationship struggles!"

What's the Frequency, Forsyth?[18]

"Amazing stuff, Mike. So darn important for everyone! How do people participate in the training? Of course, you want to make it available for everybody, right?"

"Absolutely! In fact, multiple formats for accessing this training are in the works. I look forward to everyone having access to these best practices for *living in the Q* with all people in our lives! Right now, I love training on site, in person at the buildings where people work. Creating strong relationships and a thriving environment and culture in the workplace is a huge topic today. There are many looking to figure it out, and that's why it makes sense for me to be with organizations directly, and face to face. (You know, Amazon, Nike, Apple, Microsoft, etc. Those are... companies...) This *See to Be* training, and even specialized opportunities can run full days, multiple-days, half-days and shorter. What I love about this topic is that even introductory-level information absolutely changes people! And then we have so much we can build on from there!"

"Mike, is there an R.E.M. discount?" someone yells from the crowd. They all erupt, and when things finally settle down, Mike says, "Absolutely! I'll blast that promo code on the big screen in a moment! Again, crowd volume that one would think couldn't get louder, gets louder!

"We love you, dude!" someone shouts from the sea of smiles.

"Love you too, man! I'm a fan of R.E.M. fans!" Mike responds while pointing out to the crowd.

---

[18] R.E.M., 'What's the Frequency, Kenneth?'

"What else can you tell them, Mighty Mike?" asks Michael Stipe, with a wink.

"Well, Michael, I want everyone to know that they can easily find me via all the social media channels. I'm trying to stay connected with everyone that way as much as possible. They can also find me at two different websites: **mikeforsyth.com** and **liveingtheq.com**. I can't wait to help change lives. Let's start now to be our best everyone. Let's *live in the Q!*"

"Did you hear that everybody!? The Q is coming to YOU!" At this point, people start fainting amidst the chaotic screams.

"Mike. Do me a favor--you play the cowbell, right!?" Michael Stipe asks.

"Did I tell you that!?" Mike responds inquisitively.

"You don't remember? You taught our band backstage bro! Sweden! Play these last couple songs with us, man." Mike gives the thumbs up and shakes his head in disbelief.

"And our next one is a surprise! A NEW SONG we wrote just for you, Mike Forsyth! *Live in the Q Sue!* Hit it guys!"

With that Michael Stipe, Mike Mills, Mike Forsyth and Peter Buck start rocking out to the most incredible new song you've ever heard, with a psychedelic Q flashing all over the big screen!

The place is in a frenzy! R.E.M. and Mike Forsyth have managed to turn this neighborhood concert upside down!

And the world will never be the same!